A NEW HISTORY
OF CORK

A NEW HISTORY
OF CORK

DR HENRY ALAN JEFFERIES

The
History
Press
Ireland

To Úna, James and Rosemary

First published 2010

The History Press Ireland
119 Lower Baggot Street
Dublin 2, Ireland
www.thehistorypress.ie

© Dr Henry Alan Jefferies, 2010

The right of Dr Henry Alan Jefferies to be identified as the Author
of this work has been asserted in accordance with the
Copyrights, Designs and Patents Act 1988.

British Library Cataloguing in Publication Data.
A catalogue record for this book is available from the British Library.

ISBN 978 1 84588 984 5

Typesetting and origination by The History Press
Printed in Great Britain

CONTENTS

FOREWORD

Henry Jefferies had a brilliant undergraduate career in History at University College Cork, culminating in a 1st class honours degree. He was Auditor of UCC's Historical Society. He subsequently secured his doctorate at Queen's University, Belfast. His research has ranged from the medieval and early modern periods onwards, with notable publications in ecclesiastical history. As his previous work has shown, Dr Jefferies certainly has the confidence to challenge the conclusions of other scholars. His wide scholarly accomplishments are matched by a broad teaching experience at second and third level, with a corresponding development of his communication skills. He thus brings to this concise history of Cork an ideal combination of scholarly authority and clarity of style, accompanied by a native's affection for his home town. He is *au fait* with recent specialised Cork studies and this knowledge is skilfully integrated into his work.

There is a continuing demand for knowledgeable popular studies in regional and local history, a demand which is admirably met in Cork's case by this most readable and attractively illustrated history. It provides the ideal historical context for an understanding of modern Cork. It will be welcomed by the student, general reader and visitor alike. Its author's reputation will ensure its success.

John A. Murphy
Emeritus Professor of Irish History
University College Cork

ACKNOWLEDGEMENTS

I wish to acknowledge warmly the support of Cork City Libraries for this book, and in particular Liam Ronayne, John Mullins and Stephen Leach for allowing me to reproduce a range of images from the 'Cork: past and present' facility. This resource is a great boon to local historians in Cork, and to anyone with an interest in Cork's history anywhere in the world. I would like to thank John Mullins, in particular, for his enthusiastic contributions to this book.

I wish to acknowledge also Ciara Brett, Cork City Council's City Archaeologist, for her warm encouragement and advice, as well as for the photographs she secured for me. I wish to acknowledge my debts to Peter Murray of the Crawford Art Gallery and Stella Cherry of Cork Museum for their assistance, Jim Tinneny for sharing his knowledge about railways, and Richard Casserley for allowing me to publish two photographs of trains taken by his late father in Cork in 1932.

I would like to take the opportunity to thank Maeve Convery of The History Press Ireland for backing this project from the start, and Stephanie Boner for editing the text. Finally, I want to thank Prof. John A. Murphy for his foreword which, as a former student of his at University College Cork, I very much appreciate.

Henry A. Jefferies
Derry

INTRODUCTION

Cork people are notoriously attached to the 'Beautiful city, charming and pretty ... by the Lee'. It is at once a large city, second only to Dublin and Belfast in Ireland, yet it is intimate in scale. Its main streets have a grandeur about them that many other European cities would envy, yet a native of Cork can walk down Patrick's Street or Grand Parade, or any other street in the city, and feel very much at home. On a warm, sunny day Cork looks and feels especially fine.

Growing up in Cork in the 1960s and '70s one could not help but sense something of its history. The main streetscapes, the limestone quays, a great many of the houses and almost all of its iconic buildings dated from Georgian or Victorian times. Even the dark lanes in the medieval heart of the city had a Dickensian air. The abandoned railway lines to Blackrock and Bandon were overgrown, but still walkable. There were many corners of Cork in which it took little or no imagination to envisage what they must have looked like a century earlier. The *Evening Echo* carried regular features on the history of Cork by Sylvester O'Sullivan which brought back to life stories from nineteenth-century editions of the *Cork Examiner* and *Cork Constitution*. The ghosts of Victorian Cork retained a very real presence in the city.

Doubtless, the ghosts of Cork affected me. Still, my passion for history was fired at home, by my mother who has a very keen interest in history, and by my father who has a very strong sense of belonging to Cork. At University College Cork, taught by John A. Murphy, Donnchadh Ó Corráin and William Smyth, I learnt to be a historian. As an exile from Cork, my attachment to the city has not been diminished by time. Etched on my memory is the first time Úna and I were in a plane descending towards Cork Airport. The flight path took us up the Lee, past Blackrock Castle and the Marina, which were clearly visible to the left, before veering southwards at St Fin Barre's Cathedral. Everything looked familiar but indefinably strange at the same time. That reflects the exile's experience in a nutshell.

This book was written to tell the story of Cork to a wide audience.

It opens at the start of Cork's history, with Finbarr and his monastery, and takes the reader through the Middle Ages and early modern times up to the twenty-first century. It tells the grand story of a settlement which grew at the edge of a great marsh, to transform the marsh into a great city with a fascinating history, and a tremendous future ahead of it.

1

ST FINBARR
& HIS MONASTERY

Cork takes its name from *Corcach Mór Mumhan*, 'the great marsh of Munster', an extensive area of riverine and estuarine silt deposited at the mouth of the Lee. It was an area of many marshy islands covered in reeds that were flooded with the spring tides. A thousand years ago the marshlands were still empty and desolate, when they weren't covered by water. The floods of November 2009 reminded us that much of the area is still vulnerable to the occasional deluge, despite centuries of human efforts to tame the river in Cork. On either side of the Lee's tidal floodplain there is high ground overlooking the river, with outcrops of limestone on the southern bank and red sandstone on the northern bank. Many of Cork's older public buildings, including our iconic Shandon steeple, were built with combinations of those two stones. On the more fertile aspects of the sloping banks of the Lee we may imagine scatters of ringforts, the typical homesteads of Irish farmers, during the first millennium of the Christian era. It was an early Christian clergyman named Finbarr who put the 'great marsh of Munster' onto the historical map.

THE *LIFE* OF FINBARR

Tradition had it that Finbarr was born at Garranes in around 548, founded his church at Cork in around 606 and died there in 623. His church developed into a great monastic community beside the River Lee. However, there are no documents surviving from the seventh century relating to Finbarr and the oldest known biography or *Life* of Finbarr dates from the twelfth century, several hundred years after his lifetime. To what degree the *Life* was based on authentic, historical sources is impossible to determine, and that means that it cannot be relied upon for information about the saint.

According to the original *Life*, Finbarr's father, Amairgein, was born of an incestuous relationship between a Connacht king and his own daughter. Amairgein survived an attempt by his guilty father to kill him, but was banished from Connacht and came to live in southern Munster. There he became a famous iron-smith employed by a king called Tigernach, ancestor of the Uí Echach Mumhan, from whom the O'Mahonys, O'Donaghues and many others, are descended.

The *Life* claims that Tigernach had a female slave intended for his pleasure alone, but Amairgein made love to her and she became pregnant. Tigernach was so enraged that he had Amairgein and the slave tied together and he intended to throw them both onto a great fire as punishment. However, from his mother's womb, the unborn child spoke to Tigernach and warned him of God's anger should he harm him in any way. Not surprisingly, the king heeded the baby's warning and spared the helpless parents. The baby was christened Lóan and was reared with his parents in Macroom. When Lóan was still a little boy he was educated for the Church. At an unusually young age he received the tonsure (making him a clergyman) and like all Irish clergy at the time he was given a new name: Finbarr.

According to his *Life*, Finbarr founded a series of churches in south Munster, including those at Macroom and Kilnacloona. Then an angel led him to Cork and told him that it would be his 'place of resurrection'. Finbarr fasted there for three days before a local nobleman, Áed mac Comgall of the Uí Meic Iair, came and granted him land beside the River Lee on which to build a church at Cork. It seems safe to assume that St Fin Barre's Cathedral stands on the site of Finbarr's original church because of the antiquity of the graveyard surrounding it, but we have no definite proof to confirm that assumption. The *Life* states that having founded his church at Cork, Finbarr went to Rome to be consecrated as a bishop by Pope Gregory the Great, but the pope told him to, 'Go to your own place where God shall consecrate you as bishop.' Finbarr did as he was told and returned to his church at Cork where, 'the Lord himself came down to confer bishop's orders upon him'. We are told that Finbarr established a school which was attended by many local saints, including Fachtna of Rosscarberry, Fergus Finnabrach of Corkbeg, Conaire of Tallow, Bishop Liber of Killeagh, Bishop Sinell of Clonpriest, Fíngin and Trian of Donaghmore, and Bishop Colmán

St Fin Barre's Cathedral stands on or close to the site of the church founded by St Finbarr in Cork around 606.

of Kinneigh, who dutifully surrendered their churches to God and to Finbarr forever. Many other southern saints are supposed to have surrendered their churches to Finbarr also.

When Finbarr died, the sun is supposed not to have set over Cork for twelve days afterwards! Angels came and took his soul to heaven. His body was buried, but was subsequently dug up and his bones were carefully deposited in a silver casket. Finbarr's gospel-book survived as an important relic until at least the late tenth century. What later became of his gospel-book, or the silver casket, is now unknown.

It is clear from reading the *Life* of Finbarr that it was largely a work of fiction. In fact, it is typical of an entire genre of early Irish saints' biographies that were written to enhance the prestige and power of the bishops and abbots who claimed to be the spiritual successors of the saints.

The *Life* of Finbarr was written after the Synod of Rathbreasal of 1111 which created the original diocese of Cork. The synod delineated the boundaries of the new diocese as extending from Cork to Mizen Head, and from the Blackwater to the Atlantic Ocean. The *Life* of Finbarr has St Brendan's prophesy that the same area, 'from the Blackwater to the Lee, from the Lee to the Bandon and to Beara, and from the Bandon to Clear Island [in the Atlantic Ocean]', would be subject to Finbarr and his successors 'forever'. Finbarr's successors' claim to jurisdiction over churches within the new diocese is represented in the *Life* either by Finbarr founding churches himself, or by the founding saints of other churches being shown to surrender their churches to Finbarr in person. The *Life* shows us that the bishop of Cork claimed jurisdiction over the churches in his new diocese, not on the basis of the pope's authority, but on the authority of God and Finbarr. That is the point of the story of Pope Gregory the Great sending Finbarr back to Cork where God would personally make him a bishop! Nonetheless, one should bear in mind that the fact that the earliest surviving biography of Finbarr is a work of fiction and propaganda does not prove that he never existed.

DID FINBARR REALLY EXIST?

In the late twentieth century it was suggested by one local historian that Finbarr was not a real person at all. He claimed that Finbarr was a local manifestation of the cult of a saint from Britain named Uinniaus. The argument was made that the British name Uinniaus was equivalent to the Irish names Finbarr and Finnian, and that the three names referred to the one man. However, as I pointed out elsewhere, one cannot simply assume that two or three people with similar names were the same individual – especially in a time when men adopted new names on becoming clergymen. When I attended Scoil Chríost Rí in the 1960s the principal of the girls' school was called Sister Patrick, who ought not to be confused with the saint of that name ... In any case, Finnian of Movilla, who died in 579, was obviously not the same individual as Finnian of Clonard who died in 549, while Uinniaus was British. There is no reason to imagine that Finbarr of Cork was really one (or all) of the other saints.

Donnchadh Ó Corráin highlighted the existence of a brief gene-alogy, dating no later than 700, which contains an outline of the birth-legend of Finbarr and traces his descent from the ruling dynasty of Connacht. There is also an Old Irish poem which traces Finbarr to the Uí Briúin of Connacht. Ó Corráin concluded that, 'it is pos-sible to suggest, therefore, that the record of Finbarr as a cult figure in the Cork region goes back to AD 700'. It is likely that Finbarr of Cork did indeed exist, that his father was named Amairgein and that he was descended from the ruling dynasty of Connacht – as the *Life* claimed. A book by Daniel McCarthy has shown that accurate dated records were maintained in Ireland from the early fifth century. This means that the record of Finbarr's death in 623 could well be based on a contemporary source, and shifts the balance of probability in favour of Finbarr's existence.

EARLY HISTORY

The first firm historical date relating to Cork is 682, when the death of Suibna mac Mael hUmai, the principal clergyman of Cork, was recorded. He belonged to a branch of the royal Éoghanacht dynasty which dominated Munster in the seventh century. In 697, Mend Maiche mac Duib dá barc, almost certainly the abbot of Cork at the time, attended the Synod of Birr along with others among the most important men in Ireland and western Scotland who acted as guarantors of the 'Law of Adomnán', which, among other things, offered protection to non-combatants during wars in Ireland. About that same time, an early Irish law tract entitled *Uraicecht Bec* showed that the abbot of Cork claimed the same high status and dignity as a king of Munster. The contemporary written records show that as far back as the late seventh century Cork was, 'an important monastic centre controlled by abbots of the royal dynasty [of Munster] who were amongst the leading ecclesiastics of the land – and it is a fair assumption that they controlled economic resources in accord with their dignity'.

It seems probable that the late-seventh-century abbots of Cork already governed the rich lands of the Uí Meic Iair located between Cork and Ovens. The *Life* of Finbarr claimed that the ancestor of the Uí Meic Iair, Áed mac Comgall, granted the site of the church at Cork to Finbarr in person and dedicated himself and his family to the service of the Church at Cork. Ó Corráin found evidence from about 700 that the Uí Meic Iair were already an 'ecclesiastical dynasty', though not demonstrably associated with Cork. The 1199 decretal shows that at that date, and one suspects that very long before then, all of the lands of the Uí Meic Iair belonged to the Church at Cork.

As well as their direct control of the lands around their monastery, the abbots of Cork also exercised overlordship over a series of dependent churches and their lands in southern Munster, and over some further afield. One indication of the determination of the Churchmen at Cork to hold onto their lands and riches was the pitched battle fought by the clergy of Cork against their brethren from Clonfert in 807, presumably to resolve a dispute about rival claims to lesser churches. The annals record that the battle resulted in 'a slaughter of a countless number of ordinary churchmen and of eminent members of the monastic community of Cork'. The battle fought by the Churchmen of Cork against the men of Muskerry in 828, in which an estimated 200 men were left dead on the battle field, may have been inspired by a similar dispute.

Even before the ninth century, the exalted status enjoyed by the Church in early Christian Ireland owed less to Jesus' gospel of reconciliation and charity than to the tremendous resources wielded by the greater Irish abbots in land, manpower, portable wealth and in what would now be called 'intellectual capital'. It was their power rather than their piety that assured the most senior Churchmen of their lofty positions in early Irish society. At the same time, though, one must recognise that at least some of the powerful Churchmen could be pious also.

The early history of Cork remains tantalisingly obscure. Nonetheless, the church dedicated to Finbarr became a powerful institution, the survival of which, through the challenges of Ireland's early history, owed much to the leadership of its abbots and bishops over many generations. The O'Shelbys, who produced so many abbots for Cork, were a family whose eponymous ancestor Selbach lived around 900. Their genealogy is preserved in the *Book of Leinster* and it shows that they claimed descent from the Uí Meic Iair. Eight of the eighteen names in the genealogy give indications that they were Churchmen. The last of the clan to govern the Church in Cork was Bishop O'Shelby, who died in 1206.

A 'VISION' OF CORK

Aislinge Meic Con Glinne ('The vision of Mac Conglinne') offers a glimpse of monastic Cork in the early twelfth century. It is a marvellous tale in which the monks of Cork were satirised for their failure to treat an eminent northern visitor with due care and attention. It was a very popular tale in its day and was retold in several versions within a relatively short space of time. It offers real insights into the monastery at Cork nine centuries ago.

Aislinge is set in the early eighth century, against the backdrop of the rivalry of Cathal mac Finguine (d. 742), king of Munster, and Fergal mac Maele Dúin (d. 722), king of Ailech. According to the tale, the Ulster king tricked his sister into sending a poisoned apple to the king of Munster which caused him to be possessed of a demon of gluttony.

However, Aniér mac Conglinne, a member of the monastery at Fahan in Ailech, was sent to Cork 'by God … for the salvation of Cathal mac Finguine and the men of Munster'.

Mac Conglinne was exhausted by the very long journey to Cork. However, the hospitality offered by the monks of Cork left a great deal to be desired. There was no fire to heat the monastic guesthouse. The bath was full of cold and dirty water. When he lay down to rest on the guest bed, Mac Conglinne found that there were as many lice and fleas crawling in the blankets as there were stars in the heavens! Worse than that, when the hungry visitor went to the dining area he was presented with a miserly bowl of oats for his meal, prompting Mac Conginne, 'a splendid scholar', to compose the following rhyme:

> Unto doom I would not eat,
> Unless I were famished,
> The oaten ration of Cork,
> Cork's oaten ration.

Manchín, the abbot of Cork, felt so offended at those words that he condemned Mac Conglinne to be crucified on the following day! The king of Munster refused to carry out the crucifixion but he gave permission to the monks of Cork to do it, 'for it was they that knew the wrong he had done', a judgement echoing that of Pontius Pilate on Jesus (c.f. Matthew 26:24; John 19:6). Mac Conglinne was stripped of his clothing and scourged but, like Jesus, none of his bones were broken. Indeed, the messiah motif in *Aislinge* is very striking.

Fortunately for Mac Conglinne, on the night before his execution, he was visited by St Mura of Fahan, one of the most renowned saints of Ailech. He was granted a vision which would enable him to exorcise the king of Munster of the demon of gluttony. Next morning Mac Conglinne was obliged to cut down his own 'passion tree' and, again like Jesus, 'bore it on his back' to the place of execution. However, Mac Conglinne saved himself by exorcising Cathal mac Finguine of his demon. The demon submitted to the Ulster cleric because, he declared, he was a man 'with the grace of God, with abundance of wisdom, with acuteness of intellect, with intent humility, with the desire for every goodness, with the grace of the seven-fold spirit'.

Aislinge concluded with brehons arbitrating between Mac Conglinne and Manchín, the angry abbot of Cork. They found the Ulster cleric innocent of the charge of having slandered the Church of Cork, and they awarded him his *éric* and compensation for his sufferings. Mac Conglinne, however, graciously declined to exact his legal award and accepted Manchín's little cloak as a token of reconciliation. The abbot gave the cloak with his blessing, and the original tale ended.

The original manuscript of *Aislinge* has not survived. However, I reconstructed the original text through 'literary criticism' of the two versions of the story that survive. Essentially, that means identifying the common elements of the different versions to discover what was in their exemplar, while pin-pointing the unique elements of the surviving versions to identify the editorial policies behind each of them.

The *Leabhar Breac* version of *Aislinge* is riddled with contradictions, as its author transformed Mac Conglinne into a villain, but unwittingly copied out many of the positive references to the original character from the manuscript he was working on. On no fewer than six occasions the *Leabhar Breac* writer cited 'the books of Cork' as the authority for his text. His citations from the 'books of Cork' coincide with the manuscript preserved in the Trinity College recension, and the underlying exemplar doubtless.

The writer of the *Leabhar Breac* version of *Aislinge* set out to discredit the character of Mac Conglinne and to justify his ill-treatment by the monks of Cork. He presented Mac Conglinne as a very greedy renegade cleric who behaved like a jester. He blamed Mac Conglinne's poor treatment in Cork's guesthouse on Mac Conglinne himself. He had Mac Conglinne repeatedly abuse the monks of Cork as 'curs, robbers and shit-hounds'. Even Mac Conglinne's magnanimous gesture in accepting Manchín's little cloak instead of his *éric* was utterly distorted into a mean-spirited and vindictive demand; Manchín was made to declare that, 'if the whole country between Cork and its border were mine I would sooner surrender it all than the cloak of mine'.

The editorial policy underlying the *Leabhar Breac* version of *Aislinge* suggests that it was written by a monk in Cork. In fact, the introduction to that version states that it was written in Cork, and it has several topographical references to places around Cork. The author cited the 'books of Cork' and the learned men and storytellers of Cork's mon-

astery as his sources. The clerical character of the text could hardly
be more pronounced, leaving no doubt but that it was produced by a
monk, albeit one with all the exuberance and indiscipline one associ-
ates with youth.

The language of *Aislinge Meic Con Glinne* suggests that the original
text was composed some time around the year 1100, with the two
surviving versions dating from the first part of the twelfth century. As
long ago as 1983, I proposed that the *Leabhar Breac* version of *Aislinge*
was composed in the immediate aftermath of the war between
Cormac MacCarthy, king of Desmond (1123-1138) and king of
Munster (1127-1134), and Turlough O'Connor, king of Connacht
(1106-1156), when MacCarthy's demands for extraordinary taxation
to sustain his war with O'Connor would have given a new topicality
to an already popular tale about a king of Munster with an insatiable
appetite.

Aislinge does not tell us a very great deal about the monastery at
Cork, but it is certainly possible that the unheated guesthouse with
the dirty bath water and flea-infested beds, not to mention the unap-
petising ration of oats, may have had a basis in fact and prompted the
composition of the original *Aislinge*. It is clear from the wealth of
material added to the original tale that Cork's monastery had a great
range and volume of manuscripts on its shelves, not just religious
works like the *Life* of Finbarr, but entertaining tales like the 'Fable',
which tells of a fantastic journey through a land of food – not to
mention *Aislinge* itself.

The abbreviated form of *Aislinge* in the Trinity College version
was probably written as an *aide memoir* for an oral presentation. The
Leabhar Breac version refers to the storytellers of Cork's Church community who included *Aislinge* in their repertoire, reinforcing the
impression that the monks of Cork appreciated some light relief to
their liturgically structured routines. The time is told in the *Leabhar
Breac* version by reference to prayer times.

Aislinge is full of ecclesiastical allusions and lore. For instance, it is
interesting to learn that during Mass, 'prayers were offered for the
king [of Munster] that he might have length of life, and that there
might be prosperity in Munster during his reign. Prayers were also
offered for the lands and for the peoples, and for the province as well,
as is usual after a sermon.' It is inconceivable that such an observation
would have been written by someone other than a cleric.

Aislinge gives no indication as to the size of the monastic community at Cork, or the extent of the monastic enclosure. Annalistic
references to attacks on Cork, such as that of 1081 which refers to
the destruction of churches and houses, are of no help since they do
not distinguish between the monastery and the adjacent Hiberno-
Viking settlement. For what it is worth, and I offer this as no more
than a tentative observation, *Aislinge* gives the impression that the
community of monks proper in Cork was relatively small. The
abbot is shown as a figure of authority (but he never had the power
to condemn someone to crucifixion, needless to say!), yet he was
obliged to take heed of the wishes of his fellow monks. The bishop
is shown as a figure of high standing in Cork, but set apart from the
abbot and the other monks. As a historical source, *Aislinge* has all of
the weaknesses associated with any work of fiction. Nonetheless, it
offers impressions of what the monastic community of Cork may
have been like at a time from which very little other evidence has
survived.

TWELFTH-CENTURY REFORMS

In the twelfth century, the Irish Church was reorganised to bring
it more into line with the Catholic Church throughout western
Europe. At the major synod held at Rathbreasal in 1111, wealth and
power was officially transferred from the leaders of the great Irish
monasteries, like that at Cork, to bishops who were given jurisdiction over a network of dioceses. How exactly that happened is not
entirely clear, but in Cork it seems that Domhnall O'Shelby probably
remained as the abbot of Cork, after being consecrated as bishop of
Cork also.

A number of Cork's abbots had also been bishops on previous
occasions. What was new in 1111 was that Finbarr's successor no
longer exercised jurisdiction over a far-flung federation of dependent
churches, but over all of the churches within a new diocese, extending from the Blackwater River to the Atlantic Ocean. The formation
of the new diocese must have been a protracted affair, as some smaller
church communities resisted the novel claims to jurisdiction of the
bishop of Cork. It is in the context of conflicting claims to jurisdiction that the composition of the *Life* of Finbarr makes most sense.

Historians have traditionally regarded the synod of 1152 as the culmination of a successful process of Church reform. However, in 1155, Pope Adrian IV issued his bull *Laudabiliter*, inviting England's Henry II to 'march into' Ireland and 'extend the boundaries of the Church' and to correct the 'downward course of vice' in that land. It was subsequently used by the kings of England to justify their invasion of Ireland. Pope Alexander III's letter to the Irish bishops in 1172 referred to their reports, and those of others, to the effect that 'the Irish race has been infected with ... many enormities of vice' and had 'cast aside the religion of the Christian faith and the fear of God'. The pope, therefore, welcomed Henry II's invasion of Ireland, was 'overjoyed' at the subjection of 'that barbarous, uncultured race, ignorant of divine law', and directed the Irish bishops to support the king of England in ruling Ireland and in rooting from it 'the filth of such abominations'.

One must not assume, however, that the twelfth-century reforms had no effects in Cork. By the time that Gilla Áeda Ua Muigin, bishop of Cork and 'the most pious man in Ireland' according to the Annals of Inisfallen, died in 1172, the Church in Cork had been physically changed. A prestigious cathedral, with romanesque voissoirs from Poitou hinting at French influence on the overall design, had been built to reflect Cork's status as the centre of a conventional diocese. Close to the cathedral was a round tower, 'ten to twelve feet in circumference and more than one hundred feet high'. A seventeenth-century

The medieval Cathedral of St Fin Barre was demolished in 1734, and replaced by 'an unsightly edifice' which was itself replaced in Victorian times.

map shows that the top of the tower was castellated in a manner similar to that of the tower that still stands at Cloyne. To the west of the cathedral, on top of a limestone escarpment with St Finbarr's Cave, a new monastery had been built – later called Gill Abbey in honour of Gilla Áeda. The Church at Cork had been transformed before the invasion of the English in 1177.

CONCLUSION

The earliest history of Cork is very poorly documented and that obliges historians to be cautious when making statements. The debate about Finbarr highlighted the absence of contemporary records about the saint, but recent work shifts the balance of probability in favour of his existence. Within two generations of Finbarr's putative date of death there was already a sizeable monastery in Cork. Within three generations, Cork was already one of the foremost ecclesiastical centres in Ireland and was governed by aristocratic abbots who claimed the same legal status as a king of Munster. Cork's reputation as a place of learning was established at an early date. The size of the community and the physical extent of monastic Cork cannot be determined without archaeological evidence. It would seem, however, that Cork did not evolve into a 'monastic town'. One must look elsewhere for the urban roots of the later city of Cork.

2

VIKING CORK

In 1750, Charles Smith wrote of the 'received opinion' that Cork was founded by Danes in about the middle of the ninth century. However, until the end of the twentieth century, a single silver penny with an inscription to Eric Bloodaxe was the only physical trace of the Vikings found within the city. Today, however, the historical sources, supported by a growing body of archaeological evidence, allow us some fascinating insights into Viking Cork.

No written material has come down to us from the Vikings them-selves. Irish writings portrayed them as a 'furious, ferocious, pagan, ruthless, wrathful people', intent on oppressing the Gael and destroy-ing the Church. Such a portrayal is simplistic, but it was certainly true that many Irish people's experience of the Vikings was that as victims of robbery, rape, kidnapping or murder. A recent study of Icelanders' DNA revealed that between 62 per cent and 70 per cent of the first women in the Viking settlements on Iceland came from Ireland, mostly carried there as slaves. The popular image of Vikings in Ireland today is rather romanticised. In the age of the Vikings, people in Ireland, and especially young women, had good reason to fear the men from Scandinavia. One reflection of the persistently violent nature of the Vikings who settled in Cork is the fact that the skeleton of a dog excavated by archaeologists in the city showed signs of having had its snout broken by blows with sticks.

ORIGINS

Cork experienced its first recorded encounter with the Vikings in 820, when the great monastery was attacked. Yet the annals record only three further raids on Cork by Vikings from overseas in the three and a half centuries subsequent to the first recorded encounter. The first record we have of a Viking settlement at Cork dates from 846, when Irish annals report that Ólchobhar mac Cináeda, king of Munster, attacked a Viking stronghold at Cork – Dún Corcaighe. There is no report of the outcome of the attack. Vikings based at Cork were active in 865, when their leader, Gnimbeolu, was killed in an encounter with the men of Decies. The *Three fragments* state that the Irish then destroyed the Vikings' castle. The annals make no further reference to the Vikings at Cork until the twelfth century. It is important to note that those early Viking fortifications were simply raiding bases. Had they not been destroyed they might have evolved into towns, but the very limited evidence which we currently possess suggests that urban development in Cork cannot be traced back to the ninth century.

In 914, a great fleet from overseas devastated Munster. According to *Cogadh Gaedhel re Gaillaibh*, some of the Scandinavians from the great fleet settled at Cork. We are not told whether they established a new settlement at Cork, integrated peacefully with a pre-existing Scandinavian community or simply expelled anyone who preceded them. It is clear that the Vikings who settled at Cork arrived at some kind of understanding with the leading men of the neighbouring monastic community. Their relationship was characterised by peaceful co-existence. The Churchmen availed of the Viking merchants' services to purchase English salt, French wine and other imported goods. Gerald de Barry, who wrote *The history and topography of Ireland* after visiting Ireland in 1185-6, reported that there was a stone with a hollow at St Michael's church near Cork which 'miraculously' contained enough wine every day for the celebration of Mass. More credibly Gerald also observed that:

Imported wines ... are so abundant [in Ireland] that you would scarcely notice that the vine was neither cultivated nor gave its fruit there. Poitou, out of its own superabundance, sends plenty of wine and Ireland is pleased to send in return the hides of animals and the skins of flocks and wild beasts.

Only the leading clergy and local aristocracy could afford to purchase imported goods in any quantity. Without their custom, Viking Cork could never have existed as a commercial entity.

A coin inscribed to Eric 'Bloodaxe', king of Northumbria (947-949, 952-959), was the only Viking artefact found in Cork before the end of the twentieth century.

The Vikings at Cork took control of Kerrycurrihy, a little kingdom between Cork and Crosshaven, but they allowed the senior Churchmen of Cork to take possession of all of the Churchlands in the kingdom, whether they used to own them or not. No trace has yet been found of a Viking presence in the area, though on the northern part of Cork harbour the placenames Dunkettle and Fota hint at Viking associations.

In 1118, Cormac MacCarthy led a rebellion against the king of Munster and made himself king of Desmond (South Munster). MacCarthy established his capital at Cork. His royal residence was the 'old castle' (*vetus castellarium*) found by the English on a rocky outcrop at Shandon (from the Irish *sean dún*). The fact that the English referred to it as a 'castle' suggests that it was a substantial structure. Nearby was a gallows, clearly implying a judicial function at Cork. It serves to highlight the significance of Cork under MacCarthy government. The MacCarthys favoured the development of the port of Cork in the twelfth century, and the town certainly grew under their auspices. The political and economic importance of Cork was clearly recognised by the English, who referred to Desmond as the 'Kingdom of Cork'.

WHERE WAS VIKING CORK?

Between 1974 and 1977, Dermot Twohig of UCC supervised major archaeological excavations at Skiddy's Castle, off the North Main Street, and at the medieval college by Christ Church off the South Main Street. Twohig concluded from his four years of excavations that 'there was little settlement on the south island before around 1200. The north island does not appear to have been settled until about fifty years later.' He found no evidence at all of Viking habitation at either of the two excavated sites on the islands of the Lee. Even today, there is still no evidence to indicate where precisely the first Vikings settled in Cork.

English records show that in the late twelfth century there were certainly Hiberno-Viking houses in the area around Barrack Street and Sullivan's Quay. Of tremendous interest in this area was 'the little harbour ... where small ships and boats put in' in Viking times. Its location is indicated by the location of a tidal mill pond shown on Story's map of Cork in 1690, which reveals it as extending over the area now bounded by Meade's Street, Cove Street, Mary's Street and Sullivan's Quay. In size, it would not have been very different to the little harbours one still finds at Youghal. An archaeological excavation in this area uncovered a stone wall which turned it into a tidal mill-pond in the later Middle Ages.

The significance of the 'little harbour' was reflected by a striking landmark – the 'Cross of Cameleire', which stood near the junction of present-day Meade's Street and Sullivan's Quay. It is possible that this was the earliest harbour in use in Cork. Large ships were probably anchored in the south channel of the Lee. Timber beams, believed to have been part of a jetty, were excavated on the south bank of the Lee at French's Quay. Nearby Keyser's Hill boasts a name of Scandinavian origin, signifying 'a passage leading to the water-front', and provides further evidence of a Viking presence in the area. English charters record that the church of the Holy Sepulchre (named after Jesus' tomb in Jerusalem) was attended by 'the burgesses (of Cork) and others'. It occupied the site of today's St Nicholas' church, off Cove Street. As well as providing a safe harbour, the south bank of the Lee offered solid flooding-free ground to build on. It was in very close proximity to the major routeway crossing the Lee, and the neighbouring island offered some security in times of stress.

Some local historians have fondly imagined an entire Viking town built on the island on which the South Main Street is now located, and pictures of the imaginary town have been published in two separate books. However, building on the low-lying marshy islands of the Lee would not have been easy because of regular flooding. The marshy islands in the Douglas River give an instructive impression of what the islands of Cork must have been like a thousand years ago. No one would wish to live on such an island unless circumstances forced them to.

Above left: Story's map of Cork in 1690 shows the existence of a tidal mill pond behind what is now Sullivan's Quay. The pond used to be a 'little harbour' in Viking times.

Above right: Keyser's Hill, leading to the south bank of the Lee, close to the South Gate Bridge, is the only place in Cork that still has a Viking name. (Courtesy of Cork City Libraries.)

In 1081, Cork's houses and churches were burnt down in a savage attack. The annals provide no further details about the assault, but it may not be a coincidence that archaeologists uncovered a wooden walkway, dated by dendrochronology to 1085, extending from the south bank of the Lee towards the river and, conceivably, across it to the south island, very close to today's South Gate Bridge. I would suggest that settlement on the south island of the Lee was given an impetus by the attack on Cork in 1081. The earliest reference to a bridge in the area comes from the mid-twelfth century: the *Annals of Tigernach* for 1163 report the drowning of a man who, 'being intoxicated, fell from the bridge of Cork'. Archaeologists found the remains of a jetty along the south-eastern edge of the southern island of the Lee dating from around 1100.

The oldest Viking houses found in Cork to date, during archaeological excavations directed by Deborah Sutton and Máire Ní
Loingsigh at the old city carpark site off the South Main Street in
2004-7, originate from about 1100 onwards. The remains of ten
houses were uncovered, built on a series of clay platforms, held in
place by strong wooden revetments that were designed to keep the
houses above the flood levels of the Lee. Traces were found of walls
of mud and wattle, door posts, sections of the bow of a small Viking
boat, fragments of decorated hair combs, shoe leather, shards of pottery and metal artefacts, including weighing-scale measures and
metal clothing pins. Many fish bones and scales, and also cat skulls
were found. Deborah Sutton stated that, 'We think the people here
ate hake and pike, and they raised cats until they were a year old,
and then killed them for their fur.' She pointed too to evidence that
people were cruel to their dogs – the snout of a dog had been broken
by a severe blow, and healed imperfectly!

It is not possible to tell whether the original Christ Church off
the South Main dates from Hiberno-Viking times. The first reference to Christ Church, or more precisely to its first known rector,
Stephen, is to be found in a charter dating sometime between 1177
and 1182. Yet Stephen came to Cork with the English invaders. The
last known leader of the Hiberno-Viking community in Cork, who
was killed by English freebooters in 1173, had a residence on the
south island, with a chapel in its courtyard. I have speculated that
his residence was located on the south-western quarter of the south
island (close to the South Gate Bridge, on the site of Beamish &
Crawford Brewery) where there was a medieval chapel dedicated
to St Lawrence. The archaeological evidence points to significant
settlement on the southern tip of the south island, around the site of
today's South Gate Bridge, dating from 1100, and some other buildings further along today's South Main Street dating to the first half of
the twelfth century.

HOW BIG WAS VIKING CORK?

Cork's absence from the historical record before the twelfth century,
and the archaeological evidence so far available, suggests that Viking
Cork was a very small settlement prior to 1100. One important

reflection of its small size is the absence of town walls made of stone. Dermot Twohig, on the basis of the archaeological evidence, and I, on the basis of historical evidence, concluded that Viking Cork had no town walls of stone. The latest archaeological excavations by the South Gate Bridge have proven the case beyond all doubt. There were no stone walls on the islands of the Lee before the English walls of the thirteenth century. The first of the English to come to Cork had to construct a fortified base in the town in 1177. Prince John, in Cork's first royal charter, that of 1185, directed the English community in Cork 'to enclose my city of Cork' (with walls), and reserve a place for him to 'make a fortification'. The implications of the charter are obvious enough.

Whether or not Hiberno-Viking Cork had town walls is of interest for what it implies about the status and size of the settlement. The absence of town walls of stone is suggestive of an urban settlement of modest dimensions, certainly smaller than Dublin, Limerick or Waterford, and even Wexford, all of which were enclosed by substantial walls. The limited volume of pre-invasion archaeology found to date, especially when compared to thirteenth-century material, points towards the same conclusion, though the number of mills and fisheries in and around the islands of the Lee cautions one against making too low an estimate of Cork's Hiberno-Viking population.

HIBERNO-VIKING CORKONIANS

When, in the late twelfth century, we catch a shadowy glimpse of Cork, we see that its population may best be characterised as Hiberno-Viking. It seems safe to assume that intermarriage and acculturation had done much to give Cork's Vikings an 'Irish' character. They were 'gaelicised' to some degree, as reflected by the name of one of their number, Malmaras Macalf (or 'son of Olaf'). A man named Ua Dubgaill ('descendant of a dark foireigner') who held a fishery among the islands of Cork in 1199 may have been another 'gaelicised' Scandinavian. There were Irish people, like Gilla Pátric mac Sinan, living on the south island of Cork. The intoxicated Muirchartach Ua Mael Sechlainn, who fell from the bridge of Cork and drowned in 1163, had clearly enjoyed too much alcohol, an unfortunate indicator of the genial relations which existed between the residents of Cork and the wider Irish society of which they were an integral part. Again, the absence of defensive walls betokens an openness to the broader community. Cork's Hiberno-Viking community was certainly Christian in the twelfth century. The church of the Holy Sepulchre was attended by Hiberno-Vikings from Cork.

Under the jurisdiction of Diarmaid MacCarthy, king of Desmond, the citizens of Cork clearly enjoyed some degree of autonomy under their last recorded leader (duce), Gilbert son of Turgar. His property, with its court and chapel, was clearly more substantial than those of the lesser citizens of Cork. Evidently MacCarthy employed him as the commander of Desmond's fleet, an exalted position.

Cork's trading network on the eve of the English invasion reached across the sea to England, Wales, and France. There are written references to imports into Cork of English salt and Welsh horses. France supplied the wine which was so much in demand by the clergy and the aristocratic elite who dominated Ireland in the twelfth century. The twelfth-century carved heads from Poitou preserved in St Fin Barre's Cathedral confirm that district as a probable source of the wine brought to Cork. Cork's traders appear to have made little use of coin in south Munster and that is unfortunate, for it denies us an important means of assessing their economic impact on the region.

Archaeologists have recovered large quantities of fish bones and oyster shells in Cork. There were a number of fisheries about the islands of the Lee which appear to have been owned by Irishmen. There were also several tidal flour mills around Cork, including one which became the 'King's mill' following the English invasion and may have belonged to Diarmaid MacCarthy, king of Desmond, before 1177. These fisheries and mills hint at a significant population in Cork and its environs on the eve of the invasion.

CONCLUSION

Undoubtedly small by European standards, the settlement at Cork was of great importance for the kings of Desmond in the twelfth century. They resided in a castle overlooking Cork to the north of the Lee. That sean dún had important administrative and judicial functions, and may itself have been the focus for an Irish settlement – a suggestion strengthened by an early reference to a villa at Shandon.

Henry II's choice of Cork as a royal city was clearly determined by the presence there of the king of Desmond's capital, of St Fin Barre's Cathedral and the nearby monastery, but especially by the existence of the Hiberno-Viking port. It was from this complex of settlements that the city of Cork was to develop.

In 1173, Diarmaid MacCarthy, king of Desmond, sent a fleet of thirty-two ships against some English freebooters who raided the monastery at Lismore. MacCarthy's fleet intercepted the English ships off the coast of Youghal. A battle ensued, with MacCarthy's men 'attacking fiercely with stones and axes, while the others [the English] put up a vigorous resistance with arrows and metal bolts, of which they had a plentiful supply'. The superior armoury of the English won the day and 'at last the men of Cork were beaten and their leader, Gilbert son of Turgar, was killed'. Four years later English knights went to Cork, captured and plundered the town and established a fortification there. Many, if not all, of the surviving citizens were expelled from their property in Cork and they vanish from history thereafter. Yet the immigrants from south-western Britain who succeeded them were to build upon the Viking foundations of the city of Cork.

3

THE WALLED CITY

After the English invasion of 1177, Cork became an important incorporated borough, the basis of a tradition of local government autonomy which is maintained to this day. Its coat of arms preserves an enduring image of the medieval walled city with its protective ship-gate flanked by two great towers. While little now remains of the walls and towers, medieval Cork's street pattern has left a definite imprint on the city centre's modern morphology. This chapter traces the development of medieval Cork from 1177, and offers impressions of the lives of some of its citizens in those distant times.

THE FOUNDING OF 'ENGLISH' CORK

Gerald de Barry, whose book *Expugnatio Hibernica* is one of the key sources for the history of the English invasion of Ireland, stated that Robert fitz Stephen and Milo de Cogan crossed from England to Ireland in November 1177, and when they arrived at Cork they were honourably received by its citizens. However, the contemporary Irish annals are far more reliable, and they state clearly that Cork was violently assaulted by the English in 1177, who then consolidated their conquest by establishing a fortified ship-base at Cork.

The English expelled the Hiberno-Viking inhabitants from Cork and confiscated their properties. Even the church of the Holy Sepulchre was granted to an English priory, and its clergy were replaced by English monks who renamed the church after St Nicholas, their patron. There were many similar grants by the English in Cork. The fate of the indigenous people expelled from Cork must remain a matter for speculation. Their properties were organised into burgages, and were then granted to immigrants. The surnames of the newcomers indicate that most of them came from western England and southern Wales, with a minority from south-eastern England and, perhaps at one generation's remove, northern France.

A late reference to a grant from Milo de Cogan suggests that defensive walls may have been constructed on the southern island as early as 1182, the year of his death. These walls were probably constructed of timber, and they probably enclosed only part of the south island. Yet, despite its small size, the royal borough of Cork was the strongpoint of the English colony in southern Munster, an indispensable bastion for the colonists while they established themselves in a hostile land.

Henry II sent his youngest son, Prince John, to Ireland in April 1185 with an imposing military retinue, to establish him as the lord of Ireland. John incorporated Cork as a royal borough about that time. His charter granted to the citizens the site of the city to be held of the English Crown in perpetuity 'by such custom and rent as the burgesses of Bristol in England yearly pay for their burgages'. He ordered that a place within Cork be set aside for his use 'to make a fortification', and he ordered the citizens 'to enclose my city of Cork'. This charter, with its impressive array of privileges, liberties and immunities, and the important concession of paying a low fixed rent for their burgages, was designed to attract new settlers to Cork, and to foster its economic growth.

Cork's coat of arms preserves an impression of the medieval walled city with its towers and ship-gate. Its motto signifies, 'A safe harbour for ships.' (Courtesy of Cork Tourism Office.)

A section of Cork's
medieval walls are
on display in Bishop
Lucey Park. Almost
all of the walls above
ground level were
demolished over
the course of the
eighteenth century.
(Courtesy of Cork
City Council.)

CITY WALLS

It was not until 1206 that the King's Castle was finally built in Cork – by
the site of today's Queen's Old Castle on the Grand Parade. In 1211/12
there is a record of £55 5s 6d being spent on the building of the city
walls. The work continued piecemeal for the rest of the thirteenth century. The building of the walls was extremely difficult because the daily
ebb and flow of the tides, and the marshy nature of the islands on which
the city was being built, made laying the foundations hard and dangerous. An archaeological excavation of the city walls at the Grade Parade
revealed that their foundation base was four metres wide. It was made of
large limestone blocks on top of brushwood and moss laid directly onto
the river mud. Yet the mud itself formed a thin layer upon gravel which
gave the wall considerable stability.

The walls excavated on the Grand Parade were built almost
entirely of limestone. The outer faces of the walls were comprised of
uneven courses of roughly shaped blocks, quarried from the nearby
escarpments overlooking the River Lee to the south, with a rubble
core, all held together by the generous use of a strong lime and sand
mortar. The outer facing walls tapered upwards from the foundation,
but probably rose vertically thereafter. The inner facing walls were
vertical, with stone steps at various points to allow access to a stepped
platform near the top of the walls for sentries, with a crenellated
parapet on the walls to shield the city's defenders. In all, the walls are
reckoned to have been between five and six metres in height. From
archaeological excavations at the North Gate and Kyrl's Quay, it

seems that the walls were 2.25 metres thick. Two shards of thirteenth-century pottery were found under the city walls at Grand Parade and Tuckey Street, providing clear evidence of the date of construction of the walls enclosing the southern island.

Maurice Hurley's excavation of a sixty metres length of the city walls near Kyrl's Quay revealed that they were of very similar construction. However, there was greater use made of red sandstone in the walls around the northern island of the Lee, an area known as Dungarvan, probably because of the close proximity of the sandstone escarpment on the northern bank of the Lee. Red sandstone predominated in the city walls on either side of the North Gate, though the North Gate itself seems to have been built of limestone. That shows an obvious concern with the appearance of the city to visitors. Hurley reckons that the city wall enclosing the north island was constructed in the late thirteenth century, and possibly into the early fourteenth century. Coincidentally, in 1291 a section of the city wall had to be taken down temporarily to allow a ship that had been constructed within the city walls to be launched in the Lee.

A striking feature of the area inside the walls enclosing the northern island was the artificial deposition of large quantities of gravel and silt. Hurley has proposed that floodwaters may have been deliberately diverted into the city to trap river mud, to raise the ground level within the wall by at least 1.5 metres. Drains through the city wall were constructed at about 1.4 metres from the base of the wall, presumably reflecting the level of high tide at the time of construction, and showing the intention of the builders to raise the ground inside the wall to that level. At the North Gate the ground level was raised by another 0.5 metres in the first half of the fourteenth century by the dumping of mixed fill comprised of building rubble, clay and domestic refuse, perhaps in response to flooding.

When completed, Cork's medieval walls encompassed an area of about 14.5 hectares (about 36 acres). Access to the city was controlled by fortified gates at the North Bridge and the South Bridge. The walled city was dissected by a river channel which ran under the walls near the later Hanover Street, flowed under a bridge at the junction of the North Main Street and South Main Street and continued on between the King's Castle on the southern island and the Queen's Castle on the northern island. Ships were able to sail inside the city walls and discharge their cargoes safely on the quays extending westwards from

The foundations of the Queen's Castle were uncovered at Castle Street during work done to modernise Cork's sewage system. (Courtesy of Cork City Council.)

the King's and the Queen's Castles, giving rise to Cork's motto: *statio bene fide carinis*. A Marine Gate was subsequently constructed between the two castles to increase the security of ships berthed within the city walls. There were no fewer than sixteen towers built at various points around Cork's walls for protection.

HOUSES

Archaeological excavations near Christ Church revealed that the ground of the medieval city sloped downwards by 0.5-1 metre from the South Main Street to the city walls beside the later Grand Parade. The ground was peaty and subject to periodic flooding. Generally, though there were exceptions to the pattern, burgage plots of about 25 feet were laid out from the Main Street extending back to the city walls. They were originally delimited by post and wattle fences, several of which were uncovered by Dermot Twohig during the Christ Church college excavation, and by Hurley off the North Main Street. Between each pair of plots on the South Main Street was a laneway which extended from the Main Street back towards the wall. These lanes provided access to the gardens behind the houses, and often too to sub-development comprising houses or workshops or byres. The lanes were very prone to become muddy in Cork's marshy environment and there is evidence of efforts made to provide a firmer surface through the laying down of gravel or wood chips, planks of wood, wattle and, eventually in some places, cobbled stone pathways.

A range of artefacts excavated by archaeologists from the medieval walled city. They include a silver penny, four stick pins, an antler gaming piece, a ring brooch and four copper alloy buttons. (Courtesy of Cork City Council.)

The earliest houses excavated at the Christ Church college site dated from the first half of the thirteenth century. They were single-storied structures with walls built of posts and wattle lined with moss. Some of these houses showed evidence of internal divisions, presumably for domestic accommodation, for storage and for craft or trade use. Inside each house there was a number of posts to support the thatched straw roof. Each house had a central hearth on one or more large stones beneath a hole in the roof to allow smoke to escape. The floors were generally made up of clay, upon which habitation debris – straw, moss, wood chips, hazelnuts, shells, some stones and pieces of pottery, and occasional household items like spoons, combs, gaming pieces, etc. – accumulated. Floors were periodically resurfaced with fresh clay. Virtually nothing survives of the furniture of the early houses, though layers of straw and wood chips have been tentatively identified as the remains of medieval bedding. One of the houses measured 3.7 metres x 7 metres. Another such house is reckoned to have walls of at least 2.4 metres in height.

Houses from the late thirteenth century at the Christ Church college site were more substantial, timber-framed or sill-beam buildings, often with stone footings to hold them up from the damp marshy ground. Maurice Hurley excavated the foundations of several stone-footed medieval houses by the North Gate and fronting North Main Street. The walls of such houses were capable of supporting a second storey, even if they didn't always do so. Intriguingly there were some old-style post and wattle houses found on North Main Street dating from the latter half of the thirteenth century, suggesting that the old style may have persisted among the 'poorer classes' after their wealthier neighbours had begun to have sturdier houses constructed for themselves.

Sill-beam houses were strongly built, and were possibly more comfortable than the post and wattle houses, yet they did not necessarily occupy a much larger ground area. The earliest sill-beam houses still had clay floors with central hearths, and their bedding arrangements may possibly have been no better than in the earlier houses. Only with the building of second floors were chimneys used to let smoke escape from houses. Stone-built chimney breasts have been excavated at Kyrl's Quay and the North Gate area from the late thirteenth and early fourteenth centuries.

From the turn of the fourteenth century there is evidence that houses of stone were being built in Cork, such as the two stone houses near Christ Church referred to in John de Wynchedon's will of 1306. Foundations of several late-medieval stone houses were excavated at the North Gate, Kyrl's Quay, Grattan Street, the junction of Philip's Lane/Grattan Street and Skiddy's Lane. One stone house excavated on North Main Street had an internal stone wall to create at least two rooms, one of which (that closest to the street) had a paved limestone floor, while the other had a gravel floor. Nonetheless, although stone houses were increasingly common in later medieval Cork, it seems that most of the houses in the city into the seventeenth century were constructed of timber and had thatched roofs.

The site excavated beside Christ Church in the 1970s was subsequently developed into an attractive park by Cork City Council. (Courtesy of John Mullins.)

WASTE DISPOSAL

Dermot Twohig observed that with the transition from timber to stone houses there was a dramatic fall off in the volume and range of domestic debris associated with the buildings. This may be due to the fact that stone-built houses are easier to keep clean than houses of timber with brushwood or gravel floors. Also, not only were the houses themselves cleaner, but greater attention was paid to the disposal of waste within the city.

The more elaborate houses being built in Cork from the later thirteenth century onwards are associated with better-surfaced lanes with drains to carry rainwater from house roofs to the gardens sloping downwards towards the walls. Stave-lined pits or sunken barrels were excavated in several back gardens which are reckoned to have served as water cisterns initially, but which were subsequently used as cess-pits and finally as refuse dumps. At least one of the pits could still be described as 'smelly' when excavated in 1973-4! A number of toilet seats – planks of wood with a number of circular holes cut into them – were found near to such pits on the Christ Church college site. Evidence suggesting that flimsy screens were erected around the cess-pits for privacy was also uncovered.

Excavations by the city wall at Grand Parade showed that a considerable volume of rubbish was dumped at the back of the burgage plots, where the natural surface dipped to about one metre lower than the area fronting the South Main Street and was liable to flooding. There was manure and straw from stables and animal shelters, some human waste, shells, animal bones, twigs, wood chips, bracken and leaves – the detritus of the city dwellers. It was a convenient refuse dump, and the rubbish helped to raise the ground level inside the walls and provide a more even surface for further building. A similar pattern of deposition of refuse and excrement was excavated behind the North Main Street.

Between the cess-pits and the dumps in the back gardens, one can well imagine, as Dermot Twohig observed:

> … the less than fragrant odour which emanated from such an arrangement wafting through the air on a sultry summer's afternoon to the music of a myriad form of insect life which must have luxuriated and thrived on the fermenting contents of the many drains, sewers and

rubbish tips. Such an environment was, of course, not unique to Cork but typical of a medieval town and, given its relatively high density of population, this environment must have been a contributing factor to the various plagues which swept medieval Europe.

ECONOMIC GROWTH

Cork grew rapidly in the thirteenth century, as agricultural production in its hinterland was boosted by the introduction of English-style manorial agriculture, by the new farming techniques introduced by English colonists, and also by the reasonably effective imposition of English common law, which was conducive to commercialisation. By 1299 there was a dense network of towns and villages across most of the medieval county of Cork which drew off growing agricultural surpluses and channelled a proportion of them into overseas exports.

Documentary sources reveal that Cork's chief exports were oats, wheat, beef, pork, fish, malt, wool and woolfells and the hides of cattle, together with lesser volumes of hides from horses, stags, goats, rabbits, foxes, martens and squirrels and, perhaps, some Irish-made cloth. Cork imported considerable quantities of French wine (some of which was re-exported), French and English cloths, as well as spices and peppers, vegetables and manufactured utensils. Salt and iron would also have had to be imported in significant volumes.

Medieval Cork's overseas trading network is graphically reflected by the pottery finds in the archaeological record. The predominance of trade with Bristol to the mid-thirteenth century is strikingly illustrated by the fact that 75.9 per cent of the shards dating from before 1250 excavated at Christ Church college were comprised of Ham Green ware imported from Bristol. Yet, from the mid-thirteenth century there was no Ham Green ware imported into Cork. Instead, for the period of 1250-1350, the bulk of the pottery excavated came from the Saintonge district near Bordeaux in south-western France. Documentary sources show that Cork traded with Pembroke, Portsmouth, Southampton and even with Carlisle as well as Bristol, and with Calais and Dieppe, as well as Bordeaux.

In the absence of any port books or similar records, it is impossible to form an estimate of the volume of Cork's maritime traffic in the Middle Ages. Yet Cork ranked third among the ports of Ireland in

terms of its payments to the English Crown for the 'New customs' of
the late thirteenth and early fourteenth centuries. That suggests that
Cork was one of the foremost ports in late medieval Ireland.

Cork's development was boosted by the grant of a very important charter in 1242 which greatly enhanced the city's autonomy. It
granted the burgesses the right to hold the city in free burgage on
payment of a yearly fee farm of 80 marks. It set out in detail the
liberties and privileges to be enjoyed by the burgesses. It allowed the
burgesses to appoint their own officials to direct their city's internal
affairs. It gave them a wide jurisdiction in the administration of law
and justice. It gave them the right to establish guilds to regulate economic activity in the city.

The merchants who handled Cork's growing trade grew rich and
powerful. Their wealth and status were reflected in their houses. One
such merchant was John de Wynchedon, who owned several properties within the city in 1306, including two stone houses and £169
19s 8d of portable wealth, mainly in cereals and livestock, while he
was owed £377 by a number of clients – great sums of money in
those days. He was a very wealthy man, but also a very pious individual who left many legacies to the parish churches, chapels, the
local monasteries and the local friaries in and around Cork. Two of
his sons were Dominican and Franciscan friars. Yet merchants like de
Wynchedon were a small minority of the citizens of medieval Cork.

Most people in Cork lived in more modest dwellings which
reflected their humble status. Many of these people earned their
living through small-scale dealing or by man-handling the city's
trade goods on and off the ships berthed inside the city walls. Others
were engaged in processing materials traded in the city. At least a
proportion of the hides exported from Cork were processed within
the city. The excavation at the Christ Church college site uncovered a structure with so much leather dumped in and around it
that it must have been the house or workshop of a leather-worker.
Another house excavated nearby is thought to have been the house
of an iron-worker or smith. A remarkable water-powered forge of
late-thirteenth-century date was excavated within the city walls near
the North Gate. The remains of an industrial workshop or bakery
of late-thirteenth/early-fourteenth-century date was uncovered
nearby. Excavated bake-ovens and kilns point towards food processing within the city.

Carpenters would have been in great demand in medieval Cork, for building construction and for manufacturing a range of utensils for domestic and commercial use. A wide range of wooden artefacts has been excavated from the city, and wood chips have been encountered in great quantities. Bone and deer antler were also extensively used in the manufacture of many everyday items in medieval Cork. Ninety-five per cent of the medieval combs excavated in Cork were made of deer antler, and so were many of the gaming pieces. Bone net-braiding needles, spindle whorls, bobbins and reels, and even the remains of a bone whistle have been recovered. Woolen cloth was spun and woven within the city. Some pottery was also manufactured between the mid-thirteenth and mid-fourteenth century.

Inevitably, fishing was a major occupation for people in Cork. Excavations on the islands of the Lee have uncovered many sizeable middens of oyster shells from across the Middle Ages. The likelihood is that shellfish such as oysters, mussels, whelk and periwinkles formed an important part of the diet of the inhabitants of the city since its foundation. Excavations at the North Gate suggest that fish was used to supplement, and perhaps to add variety to a diet in which most of the meat consumed consisted of beef or mutton, with a little pork and wild fowl. The finding of fish hooks and stone net-sinkers, together with the significant number of fresh and salt water fish, excavated from the medieval city reflect the importance of fishing. There were several fisheries among the islands of the Lee, and in the nearby Kiln River.

HIGHPOINT

By around 1300, medieval Cork had reached its greatest physical extent. The circuit of city walls was all but complete and encompassed the two central islands of the Lee. The walls looked formidable and impressive. They defined the medieval city and an illustration of the mural towers flanking the city quays was incorporated into Cork's coat of arms. Within the city walls the population had grown enormously over the course of the thirteenth century, with houses built not just on the Main Streets but also along the laneways extending back towards the city walls. The quality of the burgesses' houses had improved significantly and an increasing proportion of the houses

were built of stone. The roads and laneways in Cork were being sur-
faced better, drains were being installed, and the level of the ground
within the walls was being systematically raised to improve the living
environment in the city.

Just outside Cork's walls there was further significant urban
development. The borough of Shandon, straddling the road into
Cork from north of the Lee, and the borough of Fayth straddling
the road into Cork from the south, were important settlements in
their own rights. The 1199 decretal named three churches 'in the
city' – Christ Church, St Peter's church and St John's church (possibly near St John's Lane by the King's Castle). The decretal referred
to St Nessan's church at Shandon (on the site of St Anne's church
today) to the north of Cork. On the southern bank of the Lee the
decretal mentioned St Fin Barre's Cathedral, the churches dedicated to St Michael and St Mary de Nard in a cemetery which
was later partly occupied by Elizabeth Fort, the church of the Holy
Sepulchre (on the site of St Nicholas's church) and St Brigid's
church (sited on the summit of today's Tower Street). The English
founded a house of the Knights Hospitallers on the site of St John's
graveyard off Douglas Street. A Benedictine priory dedicated to St
John the Evangelist was founded nearby by King John between 1191
and 1199. A convent dedicated to St John the Baptist was founded
in 1279, but seems to have had only a brief existence. There were at
least three medieval leper hospitals founded outside the city walls;
one at Shandon dedicated to St Mary Magdalene, another dedicated to St Stephen, south of the Lee, founded before 1277 near St
Brigid's church, and another beside the bridge to St Mary's of the
Isle, north of Bishop Street.

There were three friaries founded at Cork in the Middle Ages.
The earliest was the house of the Dominicans known as St Mary's
of the Isle. It was founded on an island in the River Lee to the
south-west of the southern island of Cork in 1229. A Franciscan
friary dedicated to St Mary was founded on the northern bank of
the Lee near Shandon, probably around 1240. An Augustinian friary,
long known as 'Red Abbey', was founded to the south of today's
Douglas Street, most probably in the late thirteenth century. Red
Abbey's fifteenth-century four-storey tower is the only substantial
building still standing above the ground in Cork to date from the
Middle Ages.

An artist's impression of St Mary's of the Isle friary, late fourteenth to fifteenth century, based on archaeological excavations of the site. (Drawn by Dónal Anderson.)

Maurice Hurley's and Cathy Sheehan's excavations at St Mary's of the Isle found that the friary there was partly built on wooden pile foundations on marshy ground, and the level of the ground was raised by as much as 0.4m in places during construction to overcome the problem of regular flooding. The priory church was a long rectangular building with walls of well-dressed limestone interspersed with green sandstone. It was a single-storey structure, the walls of which did not exceed 9.14m in height. Beside the church was a cloister, roughly 20m by 20m. It had an ambulatory or covered walkway for the friars that measured 3.6m wide, defined by a low sill wall which may have supported a lean-to roof. A large room, measuring at least 15m by 6m, was identified as the refectory, with stone benches along the walls where the friars dined at long tables. A projection from the north wall of the refectory almost certainly had a window from which a friar would have read holy texts while his brethren ate their meals in silence. Evidence for the dormitories was not found, but what was uncovered is very impressive.

The fifteenth-century tower of Red Abbey is the oldest medieval structure still standing above ground in Cork. (Courtesy of Cork City Council.)

CONCLUSION

A visitor to Cork about the year 1300 would have encountered a vibrant and confident urban community which was proud of its borough, with its strong and striking city walls, reasonably comfortable in its increasingly sophisticated houses, and conspicuously pious, as evidenced by the many churches and religious institutions, and the priests, monks, canons and friars (and perhaps a couple of nuns), whom they supported. No one could have foreseen the catastrophes that were to overwhelm the city during the course of the fourteenth century.

❧ 4 ❧

CLIMATE CHANGE, BLACK DEATH & RECOVERY

Between 1315 and 1317, a series of disastrous harvests and consequent famine heralded the onset of climatic change, with cooler, cloudier and wetter conditions becoming general for the remainder of the Middle Ages. Yet climate change was simply one of a number of challenges which threatened the very survival of the English colony in and around Cork in the fourteenth century. The famine coincided with the Bruce 'invasion' which rocked the English lordship in Ireland and left English royal authority significantly weaker, particularly in outlying regions like County Cork. That facilitated the revival of MacCarthy power in south-western Munster and also the emergence of the 'rebel English', people like the Cogans who were English by descent, and yet who set themselves against the governance of the English Crown. The rebels were 'motivated in many different ways, though personal gain was always the main driving force'. Lawlessness and disorder became endemic throughout much of County Cork.

The advent of the Black Death in 1348/9 magnified the misery of the long-suffering people in Cork. Ships brought black rats to Cork with fleas carrying bubonic plague. Brother Clyn wrote an eye-witness account of the plague in Ireland, 'in case anyone should still be alive in the future'. Shortly before he died of the disease himself Clyn wrote that:

> Many died of boils, abscesses and pustules that erupted in the groin and in the armpits. Others died in a frenzy brought on by an affliction in the head or from vomiting blood ... It was very rare for just one person to die in a house; usually husband, wife, children and servants all went the same way, the way of death.

The plague stripped villages, cities, castles and towns of their people so thoroughly that there was scarcely anyone left alive in them. The disease was so contagious that those who touched the dead or the sick were immediately infected themselves and died … Because of their fear and horror, men could hardly bring themselves to perform the pious and charitable works of visiting the sick or burying the dead.

The jurors of an inquisition in Cork in 1351 declared that, 'in the time of the said pestilence the greater part of the citizens of Cork and other faithful men of the king dwelling there went the way of all flesh'. Cork was afflicted by recurrences of bubonic plagues and pestilences after the first terrifying visitation of the Black Death, while the political situation deteriorated relentlessly.

ROYAL SUPPORT

The English Crown was anxious to maintain Cork as a bastion of English authority in southern Ireland. Probably the single most important means by which the Crown supported the city of Cork in the later Middle Ages, apart from its charters, was the designation of Cork – together with Dublin and Drogheda – as a 'staple' town in 1326. This meant that those three towns, and none other in Ireland, enjoyed the right to hold the 'staple' or export market for hides, wool and woolfells. Those commodities became Ireland's chief exports during the course of the fourteenth century, as pastoral farming increasingly displaced tillage over much of the country, and Cork's possession of the staple guaranteed it a disproportionate share of Ireland's declining maritime trade. Without the staple, the city of Cork would have been a great deal poorer in the later Middle Ages.

Successive kings granted murage tolls to the corporation to help maintain the city walls. In 1368, for example, Edward IV gave a grant for seven years to aid the citizens to 'repair their walls and towers which, because the city is founded on watery soil are daily penetrated and weakened by the ebb and flow of the sea'. The walls were vital for Cork's survival. In 1374-6, the suburbs outside Cork's walls were burned 'by certain Irish enemies and English rebels'. The boroughs of Shandon and Fayth ceased to exist. In January 1381 the mayor and bailiffs of Cork informed the king that the city itself was in danger of being captured. In 1384 the corporation imposed a 'chimney tax' on the city in order to pay watchmen to help safeguard the city. A document from 1406 claimed that Cork was 'so surrounded with evil neighbours, the Irish outlaws, that … the inhabitants were forced to watch their gates continually, to keep them shut … from sunset to sun arising, nor suffer any stranger to enter them with his weapon'.

In the event, Cork managed to survive the turmoil of the later Middle Ages, protected by the city walls and fortified gates. Its merchants continued to provide an indispensable service for the region by importing such necessities as salt, wine, metal and metal goods and (increasingly) foodstuffs, and by providing credit for local landowners. In fact, some landowners – such as the Tirrys and Sarsfields from Barrymore, the Meades from Kerrycurrihy, the Roches of Dunderrow near Kinsale and the Whytes of Killaminoge near Innishannon – came to live within the city walls to escape the chaos reigning in the countryside. Such families rose to great prominence in the life of the city in the later Middle Ages.

REVIVAL

From the mid-fifteenth century, there is evidence of a revival in Cork's economic fortunes. This may have been facilitated by greater political order in the Cork harbour region as the Lords Barry extended their sway over Great Island and over Shandon, the Earls of Desmond extended their sway over Kerrycurrihy to the south of the city, while the MacCarthys of Muskerry extended their lordship to the west of the city, taking possession of Blarney Castle around 1480. That political consolidation may have helped to boost agricultural production over much of the city's hinterland. In addition, the economic recovery which is evident in Cork was paralleled by a more widespread recovery across much of Ireland, prompted to no small degree by a growth in trade to England and mainland Europe. Dermot Twohig found that, following the absence of imported pottery in the archaeological record between 1350 and 1450, 'some small amount of imported pottery begins to be found in horizons dating to around 1450'. Yet the economic recovery was limited in scale.

The wealth of Cork's late-medieval merchant families is impossible to define in terms of money. However, archaeologists have thrown much light upon their houses, which certainly reflect their prosperity. Excavations have revealed the very substantial foundations of numerous stone-walled houses in the city, dating from the fourteenth to the seventeenth centuries. Many of the stone houses may have been several storeys high. Maurice Hurley observed that:

> ... one of the most interesting aspects of the later medieval development of stone-walled houses in Cork is the occurrence of a series of substantial houses at distances of between twenty and fifty metres from the street frontage, possibly reflecting the development of rows of houses within the long narrow burgage plots. At the North Gate the second, or even the third house to the rear of the street frontage was generally of more substantial stone-walled construction. Access to these houses was invariably by way of paved laneways or alleys that developed within the plots.

From the mid-fourteenth century, tower houses were built in Cork. These were substantial, fortified private residences. One such tower house, Skiddy's Castle, was constructed around 1445 for John Skiddy, bailiff of Cork and subsequently mayor. It became one of the best-known landmarks in the city, its crenallated battlements being depicted on all of the early modern pictorial maps of Cork. Paradise Castle or Roche's Castle, at the junction of North Main Street and Castle Street, is another example of that type of tower house. Luke Gernon, in 1620, described them as, 'castle-wise and with narrow windows, more for strength than beauty'. The tower houses within Cork's city walls suggest an atmosphere of insecurity in the later Middle Ages, but they also demonstrated the wealth and prestige of a privileged elite within the community.

There is no way of determining the size of the population of Cork in the Middle Ages. There is a landgable roll for an indeterminable portion of the city which identifies the owners of 162 property holdings, mainly houses, in the city in the mid-fifteenth century. The roll is dominated by a small clique of men of the surnames of Skiddy, Wynchedon, Candebek, Coppinger, Gould, Galwey, Murrough, Lombard, Tirry and Meade. Indeed, if one takes account of the multiple holdings recorded on the roll, the predominance of a small clique of wealthy families becomes even clearer. Nine men accounted for some 40 per cent of the recorded holdings. The pattern of multiple holdings can be traced back at least as far as John de Wynchedon's will in 1306, which showed that he owned several properties within the city. By the end of the Middle Ages, the wealthy elite in Cork enjoyed a virtual monopoly of the real estate within Cork's walls.

There was a small number of families of Irish descent among Cork's elite, such as the Murroughs, the Creaghs and the Ronans, who had originally been prominent in Kinsale before moving to Cork. In September 1467, Philip O'Ronan was granted denizenship from the English Crown, which freed him and his descendants from the legal liability of 'being of the Irish nation'. The Ronans acquired considerable property in Cork, Kinsale and Youghal and in 1487 Maurice Ronan was simultaneously a freeman of the three towns. There is a tombstone under Christ Church erected for Thomas Ronan, mayor of Cork in 1537, and his wife Joan Tyrry.

Cork's merchant families formed a tightly knit, wealthy and powerful oligarchy who dominated the social, economic and political life of the city. The mayor and other office holders in the later Middle Ages were invariably drawn from their ranks. The prominence enjoyed by the elite in life was replicated in death. They had themselves buried under the floors of Christ Church and St Peter's church, and erected elaborate funerary monuments to preserve their memories. Part of the crypt under Christ Church still houses a collection of their burial monuments.

While the merchant families have left records of themselves in writing and sculpture, there is very little evidence available about the majority of the residents of Cork, a great many of whom would have been Irish people. Death, however, was a great leveller, and the skeletons of the rich and the poor can provide much evidence about the past lifestyles of all sections of society. Archaeologists excavated 200 graves at St Mary's of the Isle, and studied 216 skeletons that they found.

Catryn Power's study of the skeletons revealed that the people buried in Cork in the Middle Ages were short by today's standards: the average height for men was 170cm (5' 7") and the average height for women was 157cm (5' 2"). Their stature reflected their poor diet. The very high mortality of the Middle Ages was very evident, in that fewer than 2 per cent of the adults buried at St Mary's of the Isle had survived beyond fifty years of age. The people whose skeletons were examined, 'were

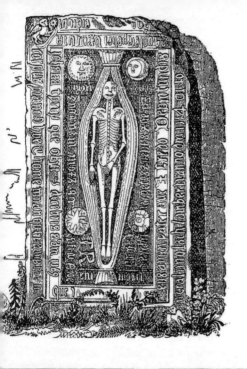

The tombstone erected for Thomas Ronan, mayor of Cork in 1537, who died in 1544, and his wife Joan Tyrry, who died in 1569.

A skeleton being excavated at St Mary's of the Isle. (Courtesy of Cork City Council.)

accustomed to the pain of rotting teeth, sore and swollen gums, and dental abscesses'. Degenerative joint disease affected about a third of the population, twice as many men as women, and shows that a great many of the people had to engage in heavy physical tasks as part of their day-to-day routine. Evidence of the effects of nutritional deficiency was found in several instances, most poignantly in the case of a young woman in her late teens/early twenties who died in childbirth, probably in labour, with her baby's skeleton still in the lower part of the pelvic cavity 'ready to emerge'. The mother suffered from iron-deficiency anaemia, perhaps due to an infection or poor nutrition.

Quite a number of skeletons, mostly those of men, showed signs of trauma. Injuries to four men suggest conflict in battle. Of two men who died of their injuries, one suffered three wounds to his left arm and head, the other suffered eight wounds to his right arm and leg. Two survivors suffered horrendous head wounds that left holes in their skulls! Some of the other trauma victims may have been injured in accidents, though the possibility of violence being responsible cannot be ruled out.

Altogether, the skeletons at St Mary's of the Isle show that the lives of most people in medieval Cork were short, and were frequently over-shadowed by bereavement, the effects of poor nutrition, infections, and traumas, resulting in much physical pain and discomfort and death. In the light of such misery and helplessness in the face of awesome unpredictability, it is easy to appreciate why medieval people became obsessed about heaven and hell.

CONCLUSION

The combination of climatic change, Black Death and political instability certainly made the fourteenth century calamitous in Cork. The economic recovery in the fifteenth century was limited, and what wealth there was within the city was concentrated increasingly in the hands of a small elite. The evidence from the study of skeletons indicates that most people in Cork endured short and dismal lives throughout the Middle Ages, even if there was some modest improvement in conditions from about 1450. Nonetheless, there was no return to the prosperity of the city's heyday in the late thirteenth century. Cork was a small and beleaguered city, and while Corkonians were safe within their walls, they dared not venture far beyond them.

5

TUDOR TIMES

In 1574, David Wolfe stated that, 'Touching the city of Cork … [it] may contain about 800 inhabitants, all merchants, fishermen and artisans'. That figure compares with his estimates of 800 to 900 for Limerick and 1,000 for Waterford. Wolfe's estimate is low, probably an under-estimate. Yet the death rate in Cork in Tudor times was frighteningly high. Large numbers were killed either by deadly epidemics afflicting the city – plague or 'English sweat' killed many people in Cork in 1522, 1528, 1535, 1539 and 1544 for instance – or by famine and disease following bad harvests caused either by excessive rain, as in 1491, or by drought, as in 1539 when the River Lee 'almost dried up'.

Wolfe's report is of interest in highlighting the importance of fishermen in the city. A contemporary map shows a team of fishermen working with nets close to the city walls in a manner which is immediately recognisable to the men still engaged in salmon fishing around Blackrock. There were also fishermen using larger vessels to fish in deeper waters for herring and hake. Fish seem to have been exported from Cork in relatively large numbers.

Not much is known about Cork's artisans, though a goldsmith named Richard Roche was named in a will proved in 1582. Queen Elizabeth favoured Cork's Company of Shoemakers and the Company of Glovers in 1577 and 1578 respectively, promoting tanning, shoe-making and glove-making in the city. The tanning of hides must have employed a considerable number of men within the city, given its role in Cork's export trade. Most of the production of woolen cloth and mantles, on the other hand, is likely to have been carried out by women in their homes in Cork and its hinterland. Carpenters, too, would have been much in demand in a city like Cork, both in building construction and in the manufacture of furniture and utensils.

Those with the highest standing in Tudor Cork were the wealthiest merchants who dominated the city's commercial and civic life. The richest men in Cork owned considerable property within and around the city – shops, houses which were rented, mills (particularly on the Kiln River in Shandon), fishing weirs, small plots of land and more extensive holdings further afield. Alderman Maurice Roche, for instance, whose will was proved on 10 December 1582, may serve to illustrate a wider pattern. He had his principal house on the Main Street in Cork with a garden extending back to the city wall. This house and other property he bequeathed to his eldest son, John, but only when he turned twenty-eight years of age, it being kept by his wife, Genet Walter, until then so that she could provide for the dying man's children. The eldest son would inherit a quarter of Mahon on the death of his uncle, a half-share in a weir in Douglas, a half-share in a mill in Shandon, and all his father's lands in 'Roche's country'. Roche's other three sons were given, respectively, a house and garden in Dungarvan, around the North Main Street, the house rented to one Dermot O'Sullivan and a share of the house rented to Thomas O'Hyallyhies, together with some personal effects and other items of small value.

Real estate was inherited only by sons, not by daughters (unless they had no brothers). Instead, daughters were given dowries to enhance their marriage prospects. Alderman George Galwey bequeathed £60 for the preferment of his eldest daughter, £50 for his second daughter and £40 for his third daughter. Adam Gould directed his wife and sons to pay each of his daughters £40. It seems that £40 was the 'going rate' for women to marry into the wealthiest merchant families in Cork. Not all women were so fortunate. Patrick Meade had five daughters, for two of whom he was given some 'Spanish iron' by his sister for their dowries, but for the other three girls he could only record in his will that, 'I have no help from my brother, John, to the same as yet, which I do submit to God and his own discretion …'

According to Richard Stanihurst, the citizens of Elizabethan Cork 'dare not marry their daughters in the countryside, but contract [marriages] one with another amongst themselves, whereby all the citizens are related in some degree or other'. The evidence of contemporary wills confirms that men and women from the wealthy families generally intermarried. The wills also show that married women in Cork kept their maiden names. People with Irish surnames formed an under-class within the city.

William Camden observed that the citizens of Cork were 'so beset
with rebel enemies on all sides that they are obliged to keep constant
watch as if the town was constantly besieged'. The mayor wrote in July
1548 that, 'this poor city stands in marsh ground surrounded with fierce
water streams that beat down, now and then, our walls and towers',
which they needed to defend the city from the Irish and from English
rebels. They declared that, 'we dare not walk out of our gates for fear of
robbing and murdering'. Stanihurst wrote that the citizens were:

> … so encumbered with evil neighbours, the Irish outlaws, that they
> are obliged to watch their gates hourly to keep them closed at serv-
> ice time, at meals, from sun to sun, nor suffer any stranger to enter
> the city with his weapon but the same to leave at a lodge appointed.

One should not, however, accept completely the exaggerated impression given that the citizens of Cork were forever confined behind the
city walls. Traders, and residents employed in processing agricultural
goods, depended on the countryside for their livelihoods, and several
of the elite felt confident enough to lend credit to lords across southern Munster. Many of the elite owned property outside the walls, not
just in Shandon but further away, in places like Carrigaline. Shortly
before 1564 one of the Galwey families of Cork built Dundanion
Castle, a couple of kilometres east of the city, towards Blackrock. The
castle, substantial ruins of which still stand, was three storeys high,
with fireplaces on the upper floors.

The establishment of an English provincial presidency in Cork in
1571, with a garrison of soldiers at Shandon Castle, brought English
royal authority to bear in Cork's hinterland. The leading men of
Cork welcomed the stability enforced by the English presidency at
first. In 1576, Elizabeth granted Cork a new charter as a sign of her
appreciation of the loyalty of the citizens to the Crown.

MORPHOLOGY

The Pacata Hibernia map of Cork gives an artistic impression of the
city in 1587. It shows a small urban centre, still confined within the
medieval gates. Castellated city walls and twenty mural towers are represented on the map. The walkway behind the parapet on the walls is

Map of Cork in Pacata Hibernia. (Courtesy of Cork City Libraries.)

shown. Several of the mural towers were drawn with cannons issuing from their windows. St Peter's tower, near the parish church, is shown with a large bell that was sounded to alarm the citizens when necessary.

The watergate between the King's Castle and the Queen's Castle is shown with a portcullis gateway, and two ships are shown anchored at the quay at Castle Street, a scene reminiscent of Cork's coat of arms. The channel of water which ran between the northern and southern islands was bridged by a substantial stone structure at the junction of the North Main Street and the South Main Street. The Cross Green nearby was Cork's marketplace, where merchants and traders gathered to conduct business. The North Gate and the South Gate are each shown with double towers, one on the island integrated with the city walls and another on the opposite shore connected by a timber bridge. The South Gate was more substantial than its northern counterpart and looks as though its bridge could be retracted in times of trouble. Some heads are shown on spikes on the outer towers at both bridges, to warn visitors with evil intent of the fate that awaited malefactors.

The buildings on the Main Street are shown as substantial gabled structures, three storeys high, narrow and deep. These are likely to have housed the principal residences of the elite, over shops or taverns and cellers. Christ Church and St Peter's church are clearly shown on the map. Skiddy's Castle off the North Main Street is also shown, as is Roche's Castle, by the bridge connecting the two islands at Paradise Place. Most of the other houses in the city are represented as two-storey buildings. A striking feature of Cork in the late Tudor period is the extensive area of open space enclosed by the city walls. This confirms David Wolfe's impression of Cork's low population levels in Tudor times. The citizens did not yet feel compelled to reclaim any of the marshes around their city, though a tower is shown on a marsh to the west of the city.

On the northern bank of the River Lee is shown Shandon Castle to the east and the former Franciscan friary to the west. There is a number of small houses shown grouped around the friary – possibly indicating a new beginning of suburban development in Shandon. South of the Lee is shown St Fin Barre's Cathedral. The buildings of St Mary's of the Isle are drawn, with a bridge and a water-mill straddling the watercourse separating the isle from the mainland. A watch tower with a bell is drawn in the vicinity of today's Barrack Street. Red Abbey is drawn a short distance from another building which may represent the Knight's Hospitallers' former establishment.

The Hardiman Atlas contains two coloured maps of Cork, from around 1601 and 1602. They confirm the general accuracy of the earlier map. The greatest difference is the degree of suburban development shown in the later maps. They show several streets in Shandon. Beyond the South Gate, Elizabeth Fort is shown, with some suburban development around Cove Street. The 1602 map shows 354 dwellings inside the city walls and 93 in the suburbs. The scale of suburban development in Cork over the last quarter of the sixteenth century seems to have been significant.

Possibly the most significant feature of the early-seventeenth-century maps is that they show the north-east marsh, around today's Paul Street, as being embanked. This embankment is called 'the walkabout' on later maps. As the sixteenth century gave way to the seventeenth, some of Cork's citizens clearly foresaw the expansion of their little city across the marshy islands of the Lee.

COMMERCE

The impression that Cork's seaborne trade in the early Tudor period was limited in scale finds confirmation in the very scant archaeological record in Cork in those times. Records from Bristol show that Cork handled less cross-channel trade than did Waterford, Wexford or even Youghal. That would explain how Cork's relatively short stretch of quays inside the ship gate were able to accommodate the ships carrying city's maritime trade. The cargoes of a ship called the *Patrick* of Cork, valued at Bristol on 26 November 1518, reflect the trade of the city at that time. The ship carried cargoes for ten merchants, five of them with surnames immediately associated with Cork. Five of the merchants had cargoes valued at less that £10, another had a cargo of £10 8s 4d, and only two had a cargo valued at more than £20. The average value was £11 18s 6d – a very modest sum. In terms of value, the most important export commodity on the *Patrick* was the woollen mantle, manufactured domestically across Ireland and in much demand overseas. Next came cattle and other animals' hides, and then fish (chiefly salmon). Throughout the sixteenth century, in fact, Cork's exports to England were comprised predominantly of animal hides, woollens mantles and cloth, fish and, later in the century at any rate, wood and wooden boards.

From England, Cork imported iron, cloth, small manufactured goods for personal or household use, and commodities used in either domestic or commercial manufacturing, and sometimes corn. The cargo of William Creagh of Cork in May 1590 included 144 dishes, 144 combs, 144 penny knives, 288 pocket knives, 288 buttons, 48 penny girdles, a couple of dozen mirrors, a couple of dozen books, two rolls of Spanish silk and other modest items, which, altogether, made him liable for a customs payment of 9s 3d. Such a modest cargo reflects the limitations of the Irish economy in terms of manufacturing such basic commodities. The low value of most of the items may be seen as a reflection of the low incomes enjoyed by most ordinary people in and around Cork in Tudor times.

Elizabethan wills suggest that the importance of trade with France, Spain and the Spanish Netherlands grew over the course of the sixteenth century. The 1569 Irish parliament named Cork as one of a small number of ports permitted to import wine into Ireland, a major advantage to the city. The right to tan leather was also confined to a small number of places, again to Cork's great advantage. Such royal favour greatly strengthened Cork's position in relation to the smaller ports along Ireland's south coast, and served to increase the numbers employed in the city, particularly in the processing of cattle, as well as its trade.

The increased economic activity led to an increase in Cork's population in Elizabeth's reign, and the growth of suburbs north and south of the Lee. However, the Desmond rebellion (1579-1583) saw the English army respond by deliberately creating a famine across Munster to starve the Irish into submission. Within Cork itself food became desperately scarce because of the collapse of trade and commerce, and starvation stalked the streets. In April 1582, it was reported that on some days sixty-two, sixty-six, and seventy-two people were dying in the city, and at least twenty to forty people died on the better days. It is a reminder that death was never far away in Tudor times.

The Nine Years' War (1594-1603) led to the devastation of Cork's hinterland yet again, and its trade and commerce collapsed again for a time. In 1600, the citizens complained that they had been:

> ... brought to extreme poverty, having lost all their cattle, rents, debts and profits of their lands in the country which was to their relief and maintenance, and are now driven to live only upon what

Blackrock Castle. The present building dates from 1829, but stands on an Elizabethan fortification designed to protect Cork from a Spanish assault.

they have within the circuit of the walls of that city and their poor trade, bearing other great charges for her majesty's taxes.

The English Crown's debasement of the Irish currency in 1601-3, together with its insistence on paying its soldiers and officials in Ireland in the new currency, and its attempt to empty Ireland of all other currencies (including sterling), caused tremendous economic dislocation and inflation. Religious dissent merged with those economic and political grievances to form the basis of a very powerful sense of alienation among the citizens of Cork from the English government in Ireland in the last years of Elizabeth's reign.

REFORMATION

My impression is that the late medieval Church in Cork was in reasonably good order and enjoyed much support from the laity before the Tudor reformations. Christ Church was impressive, with north and south aisles and a square tower at its north-western corner. It had an array of chantry chapels where priests were paid to celebrate Masses every day for rich patrons. St Peter's was only slightly less impressive. Both churches had a large number of funerary monuments dating back to 1500. However, after the city churches were replaced with Protestant buildings in the eighteenth century, the medieval monuments were discarded. Yet, part of the crypt of the medieval Christ Church seems to have survived and it still houses 'a fine collection' of burial monuments dating back to early Tudor times. They are some of Cork's least-known treasures.

There is no question but that Henry VIII's breach with Rome initially aroused much opposition in Ireland, but Cork's elite seem to have come to terms with Henry VIII as head of the Church. In fact, at least one citizen, William Sarsfield, showed positive enthusiasm in a document drawn up in 1537 in which he referred to, 'King Henry VIII, orthodox Defender of the Faith, Supreme Head under Christ of the Churches of England and Ireland, our invincible prince'. The readiness of Cork's elite to accept Henry VIII's reformation is shown by their willingness to co-operate with the king in the dissolution of the monasteries in and around the city. The dissolution campaign in Cork did not raise much money, but it gave some important families in Cork a stake in the new Church order.

The first Protestant bishop of Cork and Cloyne was not appointed until June 1570. He was an Englishman, Richard Dixon, but he was deposed after only one year because he married a Cork woman, despite the fact that he already had a wife living in England! In 1574, David Wolfe wrote that everyone in Cork was a Catholic, but they attended the Protestant Church services rather than face fines or imprisonment. There was no sign yet of open resistance to the Church of Ireland in the city. Interestingly, Wolfe testified to the zeal of the second Protestant bishop of Cork in preaching to the citizens. That bishop was Mathew Sheyne, a Tipperary man, appointed by Elizabeth in May 1572. Sheyne hit the 'headlines' in October 1578 when he publicly burned a statue of St Dominic at the market cross in the city, 'to the great grief of the superstitious people of that place'.

It is difficult to define what the people in Cork thought about the religious struggle being waged for their hearts and souls. A short series of twenty-five wills from 1567 to the early 1580s offers tantalising glimpses of the religious outlooks of some wealthier citizens about the time of Bishop Sheyne's episcopate. For instance, Adam Gould, whose will was dated 26 November 1571, bequeathed money to Christ Church 'so that the olde faith be set up'. A will from Patrick Meade bore the following declaration, 'I do commit my soul onto the hands of Almighty God, and to his mother Saint Mary, and to his blessed company of all the angels and saints in heaven.' Yet, such declarations of Catholic commitment are rare among the surviving wills. On the

Cork's monasteries were dissolved by order of Henry VIII in 1541. All of the religious buildings were subsequently demolished, except for the tower of Red Abbey, shown here incongruously incorporated into someone's house. (Courtesy of Cork City Libraries.)

other hand, William Skiddy, brother of the bishop of Cork, in his will dated 5 April 1578, dedicated his soul to 'Almighty God' alone, as did Genet Creagh, in her will of 5 March 1582. While dedicating one's soul to God alone was not an exclusively Protestant formula in wills, its use by Skiddy and Creagh suggests some degree of Protestant influence. An Elizabethan fireplace in Cork bears this inscription:

> Made at Cork i anno dni. 1586 xxiii June.
> Thy sugred name O Lord, engrave within my brest,
> Sith therein doth consist my weal and onelie rest.
> I.H.S.

That certainly made a statement about the house-owner's Protestant convictions.

Most of the wills are fairly neutral in terms of denominational allegiance. They give no grounds for thinking that Protestantism had made significant progress in winning people's allegiance in Cork, but it does seem that people's attachment to Catholicism may have been weakened. The wills certainly do not convey an impression of a general religious enthusiasm. While fifteen of the testators made some kind of religious bequest in their wills, ten did not. Of the bequests made to the Church, the most generous was that of the staunchly Catholic Alderman Andrew Galwey in his will of 9 February 1580. He made an endowment to pay for two priests in St Peter's church, and another in Christ Church. He bequeathed £3 for the maintenance of St Peter's and £2 6s 8d for Christ Church, along with a donation of 13s 4d for the maintenance of the Poor Men's house, as well as lesser gifts to St Fin Barre's and other churches near the city. He also made provision for 3s to be given towards the cost of each church being rebuilt in Cork diocese. He set aside £2 to be given to the poor of Cork one month after his death. His will reflected a very pious disposition, yet it was quite exceptional.

The collapse of conformity to the Church of Ireland in Cork appears to have been very sudden. A letter from Bishop Lyon in 1596 records that the entire population, male and female, simply refused to attend Church of Ireland services any longer. The Protestant school in Cork was boycotted. The queen's name was crossed out of the school's textbooks. Protestant services were scorned as 'the devil's service' and its ministers were castigated as 'devils' whom people hurried past in the street, 'crossing themselves' as a protection against diabolical contagion. Lyon reported that there were ten new Catholic priests at work in the city, financed by public subscriptions. People in Cork were not only attending Mass on Sundays, but a whole round of Catholic devotional practices and the administration of the sacraments.

It is impossible to explain exactly why this transformation in the religious scene in Cork happened. From the evidence of the wills it is clear that it did not reflect an indomitable Catholic zeal which was immune to Protestantism. Rather it seems to reflect a popular response to the Elizabethan government's policies of conquest and colonisation, as well as the reformation across Munster in the final decades of the sixteenth century. The Munster plantation, and the build-up of a Protestant English military and civil establishment in the south, and the intrusion of English Protestant clergymen into the Church, seem to have alienated the local population profoundly.

The citizens of Cork were forced by the English president of Munster to build Elizabeth Fort in 1602, on an escarpment overlooking the city walls, ostensibly to protect the city from a Spanish attack. Actually the fort was built to facilitate English control over the citizens. Notice the windows to allow English cannons to open fire on the city. The citizens destroyed the fort after Elizabeth died in 1603, but were forced to rebuild it soon afterwards. (Courtesy of Cork City Libraries.)

The extension of the Nine Years' War to Munster in 1595 provided the opportunity for the citizens in Cork to openly demonstrate the depth of their alienation from the Church of Ireland. The dramatic shift in favour of the Catholic Church in Cork did indeed have a religious basis, but it was not simply a religious phenomenon.

Following Elizabeth I's death in March 1603, the citizens of Cork staged a revolt. They seized the city churches and had Mass celebrated publicly in them once more. Protestant bibles and service books were destroyed. The corporation withheld its recognition of the new king, James Stuart of Scotland, for a time, and local men even attacked the English garrisons at Elizabeth Fort (off Barrack Street), Skiddy's Castle and Hawlbowline. The revolt in Cork was short-lived, lasting only a month until the citizens were overawed by English military might. Yet it was a dramatic demonstration of the way in which Catholicism had become inextricably entwined into the self-image of the citizens of Cork. Tensions between the Catholic citizens and the Protestant state were to affect the course of the history of Cork in the seventeenth century most profoundly.

CONCLUSION

The year 1500 saw the continuation of the late medieval revival in Cork's fortunes. The more interventionist policies of the early Tudors thereafter seemed to herald an era of greater political stability and order, which would significantly improve Cork's economic prospects. Cork's merchant oligarchs certainly felt increasingly confident about the future, about the security of their city against its 'wild Irish' neighbours, and about their place as civil English subjects within the wider Tudor commonwealth. A century later, that confidence had dissipated. Religious dissent merged with economic and political grievances to form the basis of a very powerful sense of alienation from the English state. The recusancy revolt of 1603 was symptomatic of a profound cleavage between the leading citizens of Cork and the Protestant rulers of Ireland.

6

STUART TIMES

The seventeenth century saw the transformation of Cork from being a small trading post on the periphery of Europe into a major Atlantic seaport. An unprecedented degree of political stability and order, albeit one that was punctuated by two cataclysmic upheavals, allowed Cork and its hinterland to develop more in line with their economic potential than had been possible during the disordered times beforehand. The city grew very considerably in terms of its economy and population. However, the fruits of the commercial revolution were wrestled from the city's traditional elite by New English Protestants who took control of the city, and kept it into the nineteenth century.

EARLY DIFFICULTIES

Following the Nine Years' War, English authority in Cork, as across the whole of Ireland, was unchallengeable. Elizabeth Fort, on the escarpment immediately to the south of the city and overlooking its walls, was manned by a garrison of English soldiers with artillery to overawe the residents into obedience. British soldiers were to be garrisoned in Cork right up until 1922. Elizabeth Fort was a constant reminder of the new realities in Cork in early Stuart times.

James I granted Cork's corporation a new charter on 10 March 1608, and extended the area of municipal jurisdiction by three to seven miles around the city walls. However, while its area of jurisdiction was extended, the corporation was deprived of the revenues it had enjoyed from the customs, which were restored to the British Crown. From 1611, royal officials were placed in Cork, as in other Irish ports, to bring the customs directly under the Crown's control. The loss of the customs revenues plunged Cork Corporation into financial straits.

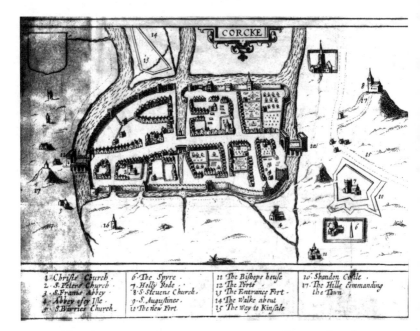

1. Chrifte Church.
2. S. Peters Church.
3. S. Francis Abbey.
4. Abbey of ey Ifle.
5. S. Barries Church.

6. The Spyre.
7. Holly Rode.
8. S. Steuens Church.
9. S. Auguftines.
10. The new Fort.

11. The Bifhops houfe
12. The Ports.
13. The Entrance Fort.
14. The Walke about
15. The Way to Kinfale

16. Shandon Caftle.
17. The Hille comanding the Town.

Speed's map of Cork in 1610 gives a clear impression of how small Cork was at the start of the seventeenth century. However, it failed to reflect the development of suburbs which was occurring at that time outside the city walls. (Courtesy of Cork City Libraries.)

On 29 October 1613, the corporation voted to raise £500 in taxes to repair and maintain the city walls, which, it was reported, were 'now ruinous and ready to fall except speedily repaired'. Yet a report in 1617 declared that, 'certain parts of the walls are already fallen, and that other parts of the same, and the two bridges, are likewise ready to fall unless present order be taken for their repairs'. A new tax was introduced to help to remedy the situation, but in 1620 yet another new schedule of taxes was drawn up to raise more money for the repair and maintenance of the city walls. Then a great fire swept Cork in 1622, destroying nearly 1,500 houses in the city and suburbs, according to the corporation, and putting the entire city 'in extremity of danger to be totally burned'. These crippling expenses, it should be remarked, were in addition to paying the costs of the garrison of English soldiers keeping an eye over the city to ensure its loyalty to the Crown.

REVIVAL AND GROWTH

The first decade of the seventeenth century saw Cork in a state of extreme poverty, while its overseas trade for a time must have been practically nil. Hardship was widespread among the people of Cork, leaving them susceptible to illness. A 'great plague' swept through the city in 1604, with a lesser plague in 1611, causing a great many deaths. Yet the imposition of British rule and the enforcement of English law facilitated major economic growth. Many local producers showed themselves keen to take advantage of the commercial opportunities which became available to them. Agricultural production increased to match market demand. Internal trade was considerably safer, and transaction costs were made cheaper by the ending of the 'protection' rackets run by local lords on merchandise passing through their lordships. Forty years of peace enabled Munster's economic performance to begin to match its potential. Natural resources were worked efficiently, and industries were set up. The result was a tremendous increase of trade, and particularly of exports. The combined value of exports from Cork, Youghal and Kinsale increased nearly ten-fold between 1611 and 1641.

Official figures for 1611 put the value of Cork's imports and exports at £20,000, behind Dublin (£80,000) and Waterford (£30,000), but ahead of Limerick (£10,000). Cork's main imports were listed as wine, iron, salt and commodities from Bristol's bi-annual fairs. Cork's exports comprised woollen rugs, friezes, hides, tallow, woolfell and timber. Cork had been granted privileges by Elizabeth I which favoured its tanning industry. James I made Cork a staple town for exporting wool. The

A
RELATION OF THE
M oft lamentable Burning of the Cittie,
of *Corke*, in the weft of Ireland, in the Province
of M o n s t e r, by Thunder and Lightning
With other moſt dolefull and miſerable accidents
which fell out the laſt of May 1622 after the
prodigious battell of the birds called *Stares*
which fought ſtrangely over and neare
that Cittie the 12 & 14 of May 1622
As it hath been Reported to
divers *Right Honourable*
P E R S O N S

Printed this 20 of June 1623
L O N D O N
Printed by I. D. for *Nicholas Bourne, and Thomas Archer,* 1622

Lightening sparked off a great fire that threatened to burn the entire city to the ground in 1622.

increase in the number of sheep reared around Cork in the seventeenth century is reflected in the archaeological record, since excavations at St Peter's Market and Grand Parade uncovered a remarkably high number of sheep bones for the seventeenth century in contrast to earlier periods. An official account of the Irish wine trade in 1614-15 revealed that Cork was then Ireland's premier port for the importation of wine – accounting for no less than 20 per cent of the national share. Almost all of the wine came from French ports: Calais, St Malo, Bordeaux, with a very modest amount taken from the Canaries. The wine trade was controlled by Cork merchants using non-Cork ships.

Cork's population increased as its economy grew larger and more diversified, and there were butchers, tanners, brewers, brogue makers, glovers, saddlers, tailors, malsterers, joiners, hatmakers, cordwainers, cutlers, blacksmiths, chandlers, feltmakers, clothiers and braziers at work in Cork. Fishing remained an important industry. A modest start had been made in the provisions trade in Cork, with small quantities of barrelled beef, pork and fish being exported. As the volume of meat processed in the city increased, the corporation decided, in 1614, to prohibit the working of slaughter-houses within the city walls and directed them to the suburbs instead for reasons of public health.

POPULATION AND COMMUNITY TO 1641

Mark MacCarthy, having counted 447 dwelling houses on a map of Cork in 1602, reckoned that the city's population would have been approximately 2,906. By 1641 he reckons that there were about 8,262 people in Cork. Such growth was only possible through immigration. High mortality rates within the city would otherwise have caused its population to fall. Undoubtedly, a very great proportion of the migrants were Irish, but there was significant immigration by English Protestants into Cork, the 'New English'. They were estimated to comprise one seventh of the city's population in 1644. English people were not welcome. They were effectively excluded from buying property in the city. With a couple of exceptions, every building in Cork in 1641, suburbs as well as city, was owned by the local elite.

While Cork's community grew very considerably in numbers, and became more diverse in its ethnic composition, the traditional Old English elite maintained their dominant position in the city.

They passed a by-law through the corporation to make it difficult to employ apprentices from outside the city, on the basis that many freemen's sons were living 'idly at home' or were forced to travel, 'for their living in other places'. Of the 359 individuals who were admitted as freemen in Cork between 1610 and 1641, only 12 per cent were English (8 per cent if non-residents and office-holders are excluded). Through their admissions policy Cork's elite ensured that they retained complete ascendancy in the corporation and maintained their monopoly of offices within the civic administration, with the exception of the sheriffs, who had to be Protestants because of the oath of supremacy. During the reign of James I, only eight families held the office of mayor of Cork: the Terry family, the Coppingers, Goulds, Roches, Sarsfields, Skiddys, Galweys and Martels.

That pattern of rigid exclusivity had prevailed throughout the later Middle Ages and into the mid-seventeenth century, and was characteristic of all of Ireland's medieval boroughs, excepting only Dublin and Waterford to a degree. It kept tremendous wealth and power in the hands of a small elite. Sarsfield's Court, to the north-east of Cork overlooking the harbour, Ronayne's Court, near Rochestown, and Coppinger's Court, near Rosscarberry, were magnificent mansions built by Cork's merchant princes in the first half of the seventeenth century, when their future still seemed very well assured.

EXPULSION

In October 1641, a Catholic Confederacy was formed to defend Irish Catholics against the Protestant extremists in Britain who had rebelled against Charles I. No doubt Cork's Catholic elite sympathised with the Confederates, but Cork was heavily garrisoned by English soldiers, and they did not join the confederacy. Murrough O'Brien, Lord Inchiquin, 'governor of the province of Munster, and commander-in-chief of his majesty's forces within the said province' commanded a large force of English soldiers in Cork. He took large sums of money from the citizens of Cork to pay his soldiers' wages, and seized cargoes of tobacco in Cork, and subsequently in Youghal and Kinsale also, with the same excuse.

On 14 July 1644, Inchiquin, an ardent Protestant, together with other like-minded Protestant officials in Munster, wrote to Charles

I to renounce their allegiance to the king in protest against any attempt he might make to reach a compromise with the Catholic Confederates. They proclaimed all Irish Catholics to be rebels, and on 26 July 1644, Inchiquin ordered that all Catholics living in Cork were, 'by beat of drum and on pain of death be expelled out of the city and suburbs, and their houses et cetera in the city and suburbs, seized'. All Catholics in Youghal and Kinsale were expelled from their towns also. The expulsions were a traumatic experience for the victims, an example of what we would term 'ethnic cleansing'.

Charles I, to whom the citizens appealed for justice, was sympathetic but powerless to help them. He was beheaded on 30 January 1649, and the puritanical Oliver Cromwell assumed power in his place. Cromwell's regime copper-fastened the expulsions at Cork by establishing a court at Mallow in August 1654 to lend them a legal veneer. As a concession to the former property owners in Cork, they were not banished to Connacht as other Catholic property-holders were, but were transplanted instead to the nearby baronies of Barrymore and Muskerry.

The so-called 'census' of 1659 suggests that there were then 3,605 people in the walled city of Cork, of whom 65 per cent were Protestants, with another 3,942 in the suburbs, of whom 28 per cent were Protestants. In the walled city and suburbs there were around 7,547 people in all. The 'census' shows that Protestants formed a substantial majority of the population in the walled core of the city, and dominated the top ranks of society throughout the city and suburbs. A charter from Cromwell restored Cork's corporation. Five Protestant freemen came together and elected John Hodder as mayor, along with two other English settlers, William Hodder and Philip Mathews, as sheriffs. A large number of Protestant freemen was elected to ensure Protestant dominance on the corporation and in the civic offices. From that point on the corporation was monopolised by a Protestant elite (with a three-year hiatus under James II) until the middle of the nineteenth century. That elite also enjoyed possession of the great bulk of the real estate in the city and suburbs. They monopolised its trade and dominated its industries also.

With the 'restoration' of Charles II in 1660, many Catholics hoped to recover their former possessions, but the king's good intentions were thwarted by the powerful vested interests of the Protestant community in Ireland. The majority of the former residents of Cork recovered nothing. Charles II's direction that the former Catholic citizens of Cork be allowed to trade freely in their city was ignored. In 1674-5, a ban on Catholics trading in Cork was re-issued. Catholics were also excluded from the city's guilds, though in the absence of sufficient Protestant craftsmen to meet the needs of the city's booming economy, some were allowed to have associate memberships on a temporary basis. Sectarian tensions were to run deep in Cork until the twentieth century.

BOOM

The wars and massive dislocations of the 1640s and early 1650s had devastating effects on the Irish economy. Sir William Petty stated that half a million people died through warfare, famine and disease in those years. However, by the mid-1650s Ireland's trade was recovering. There was massive economic growth across England, and Cork benefited directly by exporting large numbers of livestock to meet the growing English demand for meat. England's 'Cattle Acts' of 1667, which forbade the import of Irish livestock, had a devastating impact on Anglo-Irish trade, and caused an acute depression. On the other hand, the 'Cattle Acts' had the effect of forcing Cork's exporters to look beyond England for markets, and it led to the development of the processed food or provisions trade that transformed Cork's economy incredibly.

As the English colonies in the Americas grew in terms of their populations and their production of tobacco, sugar and other cash-crops that were in great demand in Europe, there developed a rapidly expanding market there for European food. Cork was very well placed to supply that market with the relatively cheap, commercially generated surpluses produced in southern Munster. Vast quantities of barrelled beef, pork, butter and other provisions were exported to the Americas from Cork. Cork accounted for over 40 per cent of Irish beef exports, and it exported large numbers of cattle hides. In return, nearly 33 per cent of all tobacco imports from the colonies into Ireland was landed at Cork in 1683, along with 40 per cent of sugar imports. Sugar cane was refined in Cork to serve the Munster market, and even Dublin to a degree. While Cork's trade grew, its hinterland expanded across southern Munster as improved trunk roads linked farms to markets and the markets to the port of Cork.

Agriculture across Munster grew ever-more intensive to meet the market demand for its produce. Fishing remained important on the Lee and in the wider harbour. Petty commented in 1672 that, 'Cork, Kinsale and Bantry are the best places for the eating of fresh fish'. Very large numbers of people in Cork were employed in processing meat and fish, and butter, salting and barrelling them for transport over long distances in an age before refrigeration. The tanning of the hides of the animals butchered for their meat was a major spin-off industry in the city. At the start of the eighteenth century there were seventeen guilds in Cork to organise its commerce and manu-facturing: those of the carpenters, blacksmiths, goldsmiths, butchers, tanners, cordswainers, merchant tailors, porters, clothiers, whittaw-ers, freemasons, barber surgeons, clothworkers, wholesale and retail merchants, bakers and skinners. There is evidence of some ship-building in Cork about that time also. Meat markets, a fish market and a corn market were put in place to facilitate the trade in such commodities. Cork's quays were greatly extended to handle its booming trade.

PHYSICAL DEVELOPMENT

Sir Richard Cox described Cork as the second greatest city in Ireland in 1685.

> The city is one main street extended at length from the southern branch of the River Lee to the north branch of it; a small channel of that river runs through the middle of the city, so that it has three bridges and it is fortified with walls round it and a castle at each end, and is protected by Shandon Castle on the north and a fort of five bastions [Elizabeth Fort] on the south …

Cox's reference to the 'one main street' may convey a misleading impression. He himself estimated that there were 20,000 people living in the city and suburbs at the time.

G.A. Story's map of Cork in 1690 shows extensive suburban expansion to the north and south of the Lee. Storey's map is sche-matised for the area within the city walls, with few details other than the Main Street, the South and North Gates and the 'King's stone house' (formerly Skiddy's Castle). In place of the medieval docks, new docks had been constructed on the north channel of the Lee along the northern shore of the north-east marsh, from the 'New Customs House' shown on the map (on the site of today's Crawford Art Gallery) towards the later Kyrl's Quay. Story's map indicates that the north channel of the Lee had become the city's primary shipping zone by the end of the seventeenth century. Story's map shows that the reclamation and development of the north-east marsh was far advanced with quays and buildings along its northern and western edges. On the South East marsh (east of today's Grand Parade) Story showed the existence of an extensive bowling green. His map of 1690 gives no other indications of marsh reclamation.

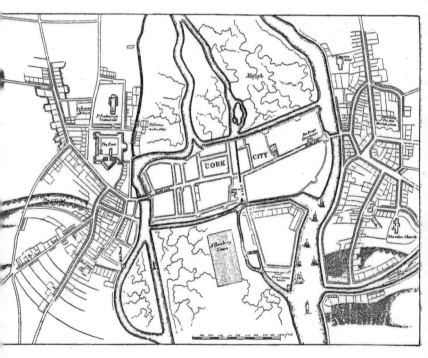

Story's map of Cork in 1690 shows very clearly the development of suburbs, especially around Shandon, which was the centre of the food-processing industry in Cork. There was also significant growth around the Barrack Street area to the south of the Lee. Notice too that the north channel of the Lee was the main shipping lane.

Yet Cork's corporation was keen to promote the development of the extensive marshlands outside the city walls. It made a number of speculative grants of marshlands. In 1686, Alderman Timothy Tuckey obtained a lease of marshland east of the city walls by the later Grand Parade. In 1686 also, Alderman Noblett Dunscombe obtained a lease of the North Strand (now Pope's Quay). He secured another lease for the south-east marsh (subsequently known as Dunscombe's marsh) and he leased a portion of the north-east marsh. Foundations were laid for the massive expansion of Cork city eastwards in the eighteenth century.

CRISIS AND RECOVERY

Since the expulsion of the Catholic population from Cork City in 1644, the city was dominated by New English Protestants. They monopolised the reconstituted corporation from 1656 and enjoyed a virtual stranglehold on the commercial life of the city. However, the Catholic James II granted Cork a new charter in 1687, which gave Catholics a two-thirds majority on the council. When James II came to Cork in March 1689 he received a rapturous reception from the Catholic population. Backed by France, James II seemed poised to at least retain his Irish Crown, if not to recover his British Crown. However, fortune smiled on William of Orange. On 25 September 1689, Cork was surrounded by Williamite forces and cannons were put in place on the high ground around the city. The city walls were bombarded by the Williamite cannons, with a tremendous amount of 'collateral damage' inflicted on the city. The suburbs to the north and south were destroyed with fire. After just over a week the Jacobite garrison surrendered. They were disarmed and imprisoned on a marsh, while 4,000 Catholic civilians were imprisoned in the churches of the city. Disease and malnutrition took a heavy toll on those imprisoned in such awful conditions.

After the siege, the local Protestant elite regained control of the corporation and took steps to ensure that Catholics would never again challenge their ascendancy. Catholics were rigorously excluded from the corporation, and they remained excluded until the Municipal Reform Act of 1840. Catholics were not allowed to become freemen, be members of guilds, become apprentices or engage in retailing in the city. The Protestant monopoly of political and economic power was to be ensured into the future.

The siege of Cork caused tremendous damage to property and the inhabitants were still struggling with the 'scarcity and dearness of good houses' three years after the 'great ruin and devastations' inflicted on the city. In 1692, the mayor, sheriffs and commonalty of Cork secured permission to discontinue the maintenance of Cork's now obsolete walls. Instead it invested its revenues in developing the city's markets, in developing the quays, in land reclamation, and in the filling in or bridging over of waterways in order to make them into streets. The 1690s saw a great stone bridge built to connect Tuckey's Quay to Dunscombe's marsh. The decade also saw investment in public buildings. A new meat shambles was ordered to be built in 1693. A corn market followed in 1695. The county gaol was enlarged in 1697. A large barracks for British soldiers was ordered to be built in 1698 in order to keep the Catholic population subdued. In 1697, the corporation awarded a contract for the supply of fresh water to the houses of the city. A scavenger was appointed to clear away rubbish and to keep the city's streets clean. Cork still looked like a medieval walled city, but it was taking on the appearance of a more modern city. By 1700 it is estimated that there were 24,275 people living in Cork.

CONCLUSION

While the short-term effects of the Williamite siege were quite devastating on Cork's physical fabric, the city's economy recovered rapidly and thrived once again on the provisions trade. Cork was absolutely dominated by a Protestant ruling class from the siege of Cork onwards, politically, economically and socially. This Protestant elite imposed their own image on Cork by obliterating the physical fabric of its medieval past and by building a 'New Jerusalem' upon it. The eighteenth century was to witness the dismantling of every medieval church in the city and the building of new churches in a Protestant style. The ancient memorials of Cork's former elite were swept away to make room for the new. Cork's secular buildings, including its historic walls, suffered the same fate. Indeed, it is quite remarkable how thoroughly the physical manifestations of the medieval past were erased in Cork. The tower of Red Abbey is the only substantial piece of medieval masonry still standing in the city above ground level. The modern appearance of Cork today belies its ancient history. The seventeenth century, then, marks a major transitional phase in the history of Cork, from the small walled borough of the Middle Ages to the bustling city of modern times.

7

GEORGIAN TIMES

From 1714, a succession of four Georges reigned as kings of Great
Britain and Ireland, the last of them succeeded by a brother, William IV,
in 1830, and by a niece, Victoria, in 1837. Georgian times were a crucial
formative period in Cork's history, which saw Cork's economy grow
so much that it became one of the great cities of Europe. Georgian-
style buildings still grace the South Mall, North Mall, South Terrace
and several lesser streets beyond the medieval core of Cork. Yet very
few of Cork's public buildings from Georgian times were architectur-
ally striking, except for the Customs House of 1724 (now part of the
Crawford Art Gallery), or interesting, apart from Shandon's steeple and
its 'goldie fish', which has a special place in Corkonians' affections.

The memory of the Georges, who were strongly associated with
the Protestant ascendancy, was deliberately erased subsequently, as the
Catholic community asserted its resurgence in the city. The statue of
George II on the Grand Parade was broken before finally ending up
in the Lee. George's Street was renamed after St Oliver Plunkett, Great
George's Street was renamed after the American president Washington,
though George's Quay, Caroline Street (named in honour of George
II's wife) and Hanover Street still serve to remind us of a time when
Cork was governed by a tightly-bonded elite which was fiercely loyal
to a royal dynasty that was synonymous with the Protestant interest.

EXPORT BOOM

In 1713, Cork was described as 'an ambitious but ugly metropolis
of twenty-five to thirty thousand inhabitants ... thriving beyond all
other Irish ports on account of its immense export of provisions'. The
export of barrelled beef, which was already well established in the late

Left: Georgian Cork was dominated by an elite who were fiercely loyal to the Protestant royal family who originated from Hanover in Germany. (Courtesy of Cork City Libraries.)

Below: The statue of George II on the Grand Parade fell victim to nationalist hostility but, ironically, its memory is preserved in the Irish name of the street: Sráid an Capaill Bhuí.

seventeenth century, expanded rapidly in the early eighteenth century. This trade was encouraged and supported by legislation enacted by the Irish parliament, and by the merchant-dominated corporation of Cork. In 1720, it is recorded that 58,916 barrels of salted beef were exported from Cork. Charles Smith, quoting from the Cork Custom House books, reported that exports of beef numbered 118,306 barrels in 1744. Not surprisingly, one contemporary described Cork as the 'slaughterhouse of Ireland'. In the early 1740s, Cork may have accounted for almost three quarters of all of Ireland's beef exports. This meat was exported to ports across western Europe, but mostly to the British colonies in North America and the West Indies. Pork, too, was salted and barrelled in Cork for export. This trade expanded from 6,264 barrels in 1720 to 10,360 barrels in 1741.

An important by-product of beef and pork processing was tallow, which was widely used to make candles and soap. Much of the tallow produced in Cork was exported. Cattle hides were another valuable by-product of the meat-processing industry. Exports of raw hides from Cork numbered 23,032 in 1720 and fluctuated upwards towards 50,750 in 1744. Exports of tanned hide were much smaller in volume, a fact which Smith accounted for by referring to the lack of local oak bark for tanning.

Salted butter was, after beef, Cork's most important export commodity in the eighteenth century. This industry was strictly regulated to promote its development. Butter brought to Cork from dairy farms across Munster was officially tested, weighed and branded before it could be put onto the market. In 1720, 71,485 cwt of salted butter were exported from Cork, rising to 97,852 cwt in 1744. This comprised about half of all of Ireland's butter exports in the early 1740s.

Cork's Company of Brewers was incorporated by a royal charter in 1743, which suggests that brewing had already emerged as a significant industry within the city. As Cork's provisions trade in butter, beef and pork grew, as well as a growing herring trade, not to mention brewing, so too did coopering. The Company of Coopers in Cork was incorporated in 1701. They provided the timber barrels in which beer and salted provisions were stored.

There were two short-lived sail-cloth factories established at Dunkettle, near Cork, but they do not appear to have survived much beyond 1725. On the other hand, in 1726 a substantial sail-cloth industry was founded at Douglas. By the mid-eighteenth century it had 100 looms in operation and employed a total of 750 people at various stages of the manufacturing process. The sail-cloth industry prospered as Cork's maritime trade expanded.

Most manufacturing in Cork in the early eighteenth century was carried out in small-scale enterprises geared to the domestic market, and collectively those concerns employed thousands of men, women and children. In addition, there would have been hundreds of men involved in loading and unloading vessels, and in other transportation tasks, and countless men, women and children engaged in small-scale vending. The woollen industry was still dispersed in homes across the countryside in the early eighteenth century, but woollen cloth production was increasingly concentrated in factories in the city as the century progressed.

To encourage Cork's economic development, the merchants who dominated its corporation adopted a pro-active role in developing the city's commercial infrastructure. In 1703, the corporation secured an Act of parliament to improve shipping access to the city quays. The north channel of the Lee was dredged as far as the North Gate Bridge. In 1710, the corporation built a new Exchange at the junction of Castle Street and the Main Street. Designed by an Italian architect with a facade of classical columns, it was considered 'the noblest and most regular building of its kind in Ireland'.

In 1712 and 1713, the North Gate Bridge and South Gate Bridge were built to improve vehicular access to the city centre. From 1721 crane houses, public weighing houses for butter and tallow, were erected in Shandon by the corporation to improve the regulation of those trades. In 1733, meat and milk markets were established at Barrack Street on the south side of Cork. In 1739, the city's main cattle market was replaced by a much more spacious facility on a two-and-a-half-acre site just north of Blarney Street. Shandon was the main industrial centre in Cork, with many slaughter houses built around the cattle market, and yards for salting and packing meat and butter, as well as cooperage yards and tanning yards. In 1740, a new Corn Market, 'a large commodious edifice erected on pillars of the Tuscan order, of hewn stone', was built on Cornmarket Street.

Cork's population grew from an estimated 41,000 in 1750 to a striking 80,000 by 1821. That population surge suggests an acceleration of Cork's economic fortunes from the late eighteenth century into the early nineteenth century. Exports of beef, butter and pork increased throughout the second half of the eighteenth century. Cork

Castle Street, with the Exchange, built in 1710, shown on the left.

Nathaniel Grogan's sketch of the North Gate Bridge in about 1770. This was the only bridge into the city centre from the north until 1789 and Grogan makes it clear how very narrow it was. (Courtesy of Cork City Libraries.)

also developed a major herring export industry. The revolutionary wars from 1776 caused disruption to international trade that led to a great contraction in exports to mainland Europe, but an increase in trade to Britain. The sale of provisions to the British military forces during the Napoleonic Wars helped significantly to compensate for the loss of overseas markets. Nonetheless, Cork's economic and population surge did not depend on provisions alone.

From the late eighteenth century, employment opportunities in the textile industry increased dramatically. David Dickson reckons that between 15,000 and 20,000 spinners were employed in the Cork region catering for the export market, and another 4,000 to 5,000 catering for the domestic market. In 1800, there were forty-one companies engaged in woollen manufacturing in the city, with 2,500 employees. Cork exported 300,000 yards of woollen yarn per annum. The linen industry also expanded greatly in Cork. Linen found a ready outlet in the local sail-cloth industry, but exports of linen cloth were also very considerable, increasing from 280,000 yards in 1780 to 1,540,000 yards in 1816. Cotton production also flourished. Henry and James Sadlier founded a large cotton business at Glasheen in 1781, which employed 1,000 people. Five years later the Sadlier brothers had four factories, employing 8,000 people in all.

In fact, Cork became a major industrial centre. Spin-off industries which grew out of textiles included not only the large sail-cloth industry at Douglas, but a sizeable clothing industry geared mainly to the large and growing domestic market in Cork and its hinterland. Carpets were manufactured in Cork. Glove-making provided work for 3,000 women in 1800. Hat-making employed another 120 people in 1800, while there were 200 hosiery frames in the city providing hundreds of other jobs. Much of the leather produced by Cork's tanning industry was used by the local footwear industry. Tallow produced in Cork was used increasingly for the local manufacture of candles and soap. There were thousands of people employed in small-scale craft industries and what would now be called service industries in the city, while the construction industry was very busy throughout this period. Cork also boasted paper mills and a significant glass-making industry in the late eighteenth century.

Two of Cork's chief 'success stories' in the late Georgian times were the brewing and distilling industries. The growth of these industries is a good reflection of rising living standards in the Cork region at that time. There were ten distilleries in Cork in 1796, with a total capacity of 11,000 gallons. That capacity was greatly expanded. By 1812, Mr Walker, the 'greatest distiller' in Ireland, produced 17,000 gallons of whiskey a week in one plant, while another Cork plant produced 9,000 gallons a week. Cork whiskey provided a sizeable market for locally grown corn, which generated incomes for farmers, carters and coopers, apart altogether from the hundreds of men employed directly in the distilleries. The brewing industry also grew considerably in Cork in the late eighteenth century. Beamish & Crawford's brewery was founded in 1792, and it was Ireland's largest brewery until 1833. In 1805, 150,000 gallons of beer were brewed in Cork by eight or nine breweries. By 1812 Beamish & Crawford alone was producing 100,000 gallons of beer per annum.

Cork may be described as an industrial city by the end of the eighteenth century. However, Cork was handicapped by the absence of coal in its hinterland, for European experience shows that industry in the nineteenth century normally prospered close to coalfields. Also, much of Cork's industrial output was geared to the domestic Irish market, which at the time was insulated from foreign competition by a system of tariffs. Once those tariffs were dismantled under the terms of the Act of Union, mainly in 1824, many of Cork's industries were unable to withstand the brunt of British competition. That competition had a devastating effect on Cork's economy. Nonetheless, it has to be emphasised that up to 1815 no one could reasonably have imagined that the prosperity enjoyed in Cork in the eighteenth century would end quite so severely.

LIFE IN CORK

The mayor of Cork was elected on 29 September each year. It was an extremely busy time of the year in Georgian Cork because September saw the start of the slaughtering season. The roads into Cork were crowded, as about 80,000 bullocks were brought to the north side of the city for butchering. The smell of cattle dung, blood, guts and rotting flesh was everywhere. The cries of animals being killed filled the air. It was a hectic time, with exhausting twelve-hour shifts being normal at the slaughter houses, the salting, tanning, tallow-making and cooperage yards. On the other hand, it was a time when jobs were readily available and large numbers of young adults were drawn into the city for seasonal work.

It was a time, too, when vast amounts of cheap offal was available to the poor; the tripe and drisheen which graced tables in the crowded tenements and in the small single-storey houses of the poor around the edges of Cork. Tripe is part of the stomach of a cow or sheep and needs hours of boiling to make it edible. Drisheen is a type of black pudding made from a mixture of animal blood, milk, salt, fat and breadcrumbs, which is cooked using an animal's intestine as the sausage skin. As the cattle killing drew to a close towards the end of the year, the season began for the pigs, another round of blood-letting and squealing, and the poor could feast on crubeens – pigs' trotters – sometimes boiled with cabbage. The slaughtering season marked the culinary high point of many a Cork family's year!

After the meat processing was completed and the seasonal migrants returned to the countryside, life in the city grew quieter. The winter rains sometimes held people's attention, because when the Lee flooded, as happened often, it could wash away some of the quay walls and buildings on the low-lying islands. Lent was meat-free for the poor, and not always solely because of religious convictions. Depending on the weather of the previous summer and autumn, and its effects on the harvest, early summer might be a time of food shortage. Nonetheless, by May each year the roads into Cork were growing busy again as pack-horses from dairy farms right across southern Munster brought butter to the market at Shandon for processing. It was a busy trade, and mercifully peaceful and less odorous.

Cork was not a healthy place to live in in Georgian times. The growing population was concentrated in a confined area, and much of it was housed in tenements along narrow, fetid lanes off the Main Street, off Shandon Street or Barrack Street. The city, and especially the northern suburbs, stank with the detritus of the meat trade; excrement, spilled blood and guts. Human waste, natural and domestic, covered streets and lanes everywhere and spilled out onto neighbouring open spaces. The many smaller channels of the Lee were little more than open sewers, and yet contemporary commentators were often shocked to see many of the poor draw their drinking water from the Lee at low tide in dry summer times. Inevitably, such insanitary conditions proved to be a breeding ground for disease, especially when personal hygiene habits were very rudimentary.

The swearing in of a new mayor of Cork was a time of public celebration and revelry. (Courtesy of Cork City Libraries.)

Bad weather could have disastrous consequences for the poor. In 1738, heavy rain affected the corn and potato harvests, leading to increased food prices, and a contraction of the domestic market for manufactured goods which then led to increased unemployment. The 'great frost of 1739' devastated the potato harvest and caused malnutrition in Cork that facilitated the spread of disease. In the late summer of 1740, 'gripping diarrhoeas and an epidemic of dysenteries broke out which … caused great and incredible mortality during all the ensuing winter'. The famine of 1740 may have killed more people in Cork than the Great Famine of 1845-50. Remarkably, though, the death rate in Cork was reduced over the course of Georgian times. Eating animal offal was reckoned to have caused repeated epidemics of sickness at the start of the century, but after 1721, probably because of greater care in boiling them for long enough, the offal epidemics 'began to dwindle in their effects, and by degrees totally disappeared'.

A modest start was made in providing public health care, though it remained very rudimentary before Victorian times. In 1719, the foundations of the North Charitable Hospital were laid down in Shandon. It was maintained by private charity. In 1750, this institution, known as the North Infirmary, had only six beds for patients, but it treated up to 2,000 patients a year on an 'out-patient' basis. The South Infirmary was opened in 1762 off Infirmary Road. From 1771, each of the hospitals was granted an annual sum of £100 by Cork Corporation and the Grand Jury towards their operation. In 1787, a Dispensary and Humane Society was established at Hanover Street which gave free medical care to the poor of Cork, with a medical officer and ancillary staff appointed for each of seven districts in the city. In 1798, the Lying-in Hospital at Mardyke Street was opened, with twelve beds. The provision of health care in the city in the eighteenth century remained woefully inadequate, but as people's living standards and their diets improved, and as vaccination against smallpox became general, people's health got better and most lived a little longer.

Provision for the poor remained a matter for private charity in the first half of the eighteenth century. In 1718, Skiddy's and Brettridge's Almshouse was transferred from within the medieval city walls to new premises close to Shandon church. In 1719, one Captain T. Deane founded an almshouse for eight poor people, together with a school for forty pupils, on the north-east marsh. Those almshouses were small and almost exclusively Protestant. A Foundling Hospital was opened in 1747 to house abandoned babies. Cork's first purpose-built lunatic asylum was opened in 1791.

For the generality of the poor there was little more than nominal assistance until the House of Industry was opened in 1776 – the precursor of Cork's Victorian workhouse. A cynic might quip that the institution was designed to salve the consciences of the wealthy by reassuring them that the most absolutely destitute were provided with a frugal refuge at an affordable price. It was certainly no panacea for the poverty which prevailed in the city slums. Indeed, throughout the eighteenth century there were many occasions when food shortages drove some of the poor to resort to rioting in order to force the elite to take some action to alleviate their plight.

The provision of clean water would have made a major contribution to public health. However, none of the wealthy were keen to pay the tax needed to provide it. In 1761 an Act of parliament was passed to establish Cork's Pipe Water Company. It was a commercial venture funded by a joint investment of capital by the corporation (25 per cent) and private interests (75 per cent). It provided clean water taken from the Lee and pumped to customers through pipes made of beech or larch. However, water could only be supplied to low-lying parts of the city, and then at a considerable charge. Only one public fountain was erected to supply free water to the poor, to ensure that anyone who wanted clean water would have to pay a high price for it. No other public fountain was erected in Cork until 1845. Into the early years of the nineteenth century, poor people were still to be seen in Cork collecting rainwater falling from roofs, or taking water from the Lee and even from the gutters on the streets.

Needless to say, there were no sewers in Georgian Cork to carry away human urine or excrement. There was some small attention paid to the streets of Cork by the corporation from 1761, with the introduction of new regulations requiring the streets to be swept at least three times a week. Yet, into Victorian times visitors found Cork to be a dirty city. In 1765, Cork's Wide Streets Commissioners were established to widen some of the main thoroughfares through the city. That work took a great deal of time because finance was very limited. Nonetheless, progress was made in widening the Main Street, Castle Street, Tuckey Street and the bottom of Shandon Street, while its greatest achievement, the creation of Great George's Street (now Washington Street), was completed in 1836.

The flood waters of the Lee rushing past the Courthouse on Great George's Street in 1853. A similar scene was repeated in November 2009. (Courtesy of Cork City Libraries.)

An Act of parliament in 1719 directed that street lights be provided in Dublin, Cork and Limerick. However, those responsible for the lights in Cork were 'none too scrupulous', though Cork's many river channels posed a particular hazard to anyone walking about at night. In 1763, an Act was passed directing, among other things, that walls and railings be erected on the quaysides in order to reduce the number of deaths by drowning. It was not until 1771 that an Act of parliament imposed a property tax in Cork to pay for street lighting. By 1799 there were 2,188 street lamps in the city. From 1825, gas was used to light Cork's streets after dark. Very slowly but surely the city was taking on a more modern appearance.

RELIGION AND POLITICS

As Cork's commerce and industry grew, so too did its population, much of it due to immigration from England. To cater for the growing number of Protestants, a number of churches were built in Cork in the Georgian times. A Huguenot chapel was built in 1712 on the north-east marsh, on what became French Church Street. A Presbyterian chapel was built on Dunscombe's marsh, at Prince's Street, in 1717. The Quakers had their meeting house on Hammond's marsh, to the west of the medieval city. In 1752, a Methodist meeting house was built nearby on what became Henry Street.

Cork's merchant elite were, overwhelmingly, members of the Church of Ireland. They used their positions on Cork's corporation to secure an Act of parliament in 1719 to enable them to levy a duty on coal to pay for the building of a new Christ Church on the South Main Street. Christ Church was the civic church of the city. The coal levy was extended to pay for the building of St Paul's church at Paul Street, and St Anne's church, Shandon, which was built in 1722, with its famous steeple added in 1749. St Mary's church, Shandon, had been built in 1693 near the foot of Shandon Street across from Blarney Street, to serve the growing population there. St Nicholas's church was built in 1722 to serve the southern suburbs. It was replaced by a more impressive limestone church in 1849-50. The medieval Cathedral of St Fin Barre was demolished in 1734, and replaced by 'an unsightly edifice' which was also replaced in Victorian times. St Peter's church on the North Main Street was demolished in 1782 and replaced in 1785.

Above left: The Huguenot burial ground off Carey's Lane. (Courtesy of John Mullins.)

Above right: St Fin Barre's Cathedral, 'an unsightly edifice' built in 1734 to replace its medieval predecessor. (Courtesy of Cork City Libraries.)

The 1834 religious census revealed that there were 16,899 Protestants in the city parishes. Protestants are reckoned to have comprised 12 per cent of Cork's overall population in 1831, but in the parishes of Christ Church and St Peter's, Protestants comprised one third of the residents, and 20.7 per cent of those in St Paul's parish. That concentration of Protestants on the islands of the Lee was a legacy of the 'siege mentality' from Stuart times.

After the catastrophic setbacks of the seventeenth century, the eighteenth century witnessed a very gradual improvement in the fortunes of Cork's Catholic community. Catholics were denied the franchise at local and national levels, and were excluded from membership of Cork's corporation as well as the Irish parliament. They were also barred from full membership of Cork's trade and craft guilds. However, the rapid expansion of the city's economy in the eighteenth century made it impossible to exclude Catholics altogether from Cork's business life. Despite the best efforts of the Protestant corporation, some Catholics managed to gain a share of the city's growing wealth, especially in the butter trade. By the mid-eighteenth century, the emerging Catholic elite began to feel confident enough to challenge the Protestant ascendancy in the city. Their progress is illustrated by the fact that Cork's Committee of Merchants, founded in 1769, included from the beginning both Catholic and Protestant members.

There were only four Catholic priests in Cork in 1704, and no church. In 1729, however, the North Chapel (on the site of St Mary's Cathedral), and the South Chapel (on the site of St Finbarr's South church) were built. In 1786, a modest parish church dedicated to SS Peter and Paul was built at Carey's Lane, off Patrick Street. These three parish churches could not possibly accommodate the burgeoning Catholic population of Cork, but the ministry of the parish clergy was complemented by that of a number of orders of friars, especially from the mid-eighteenth century.

Dominican friars seem to have maintained a presence in Cork despite the Williamite revolution. They established a house at Friary Lane, off Shandon Street in 1784. An Augustinian house was established at Fishamble Lane in 1741, before the community transferred to larger premises at Brunswick Street in 1780. The Franciscans' house at Broad Lane is shown on Rocque's map of Cork in 1759. In 1771, they established a larger friary at Little Castle Street. In 1760, Capuchins came to Cork. In 1771, they built a friary at Blackmoor Lane behind Sullivan's Quay. Also in 1771, the Ursuline Sisters established a convent at Blackrock for the education of the daughters of the more prosperous Catholic families in the city. Poorer girls were offered an education by the Presentation Sisters, a new order of nuns founded by Nano Nagle in Cork, at the South Presentation Convent (opened in 1775) and the North Presentation Convent (opened in 1799). The Presentation Brothers and Christian Brothers, inspired by Nano Nagle, established similar schools for boys in Cork in the early nineteenth century.

Anti-Catholic feeling was particularly strong in Cork during the penal days. A tightly bonded clique of Protestant merchant and professional men in the city formed the Friendly Club, which virtually monopolised the corporation. The club controlled the membership of the common council of Cork's corporation, and decided who could become a freeman of the city. A government inquiry in 1833 revealed that only 73 of the city's more than 1,600 freemen were Catholics and none had been elected since 1825. The senior sheriff of Cork was invariably the club's president. The mayors were chosen from the ranks of former sheriffs. Club members controlled the distribution of jobs in the corporation, and they paid themselves very well. Between a third and a half of the corporation's revenues was paid in generous salaries to its employees. The Brunswick Club and the Orange Order were both very active in Cork, with members who were more than keen to preserve the Protestant ascendancy in Cork against a rising tide of democratic sentiment.

Even after legislation was enacted to allow Catholics to vote from 1793, Cork's corporation kept enrolling additional Protestant freemen in the city to cancel the effects of the increasing numbers of Catholic voters. The corrupt practices of the corporation and the vote-rigging it engaged in caused a lot of ill feeling in the city, and heightened Catholics' sense of injustice. Catholic businessmen, together with some liberal Protestants in Cork, formed themselves into a Chamber of Commerce in 1819, a body which was explicitly non-sectarian but supported the granting of civil rights to Catholics, what was popularly termed 'Catholic emancipation'. Cork had its own committee of the Catholic Association from April 1824. Yet it was not until Westminster enacted the Municipal Corporations Act of 1840 that the power of the Friendly Club was broken in Cork. In 1841 Thomas Lyons was elected as the first Catholic mayor of Cork since the reign of James II.

The success of Cork's Catholic middle classes in wresting control of the corporation from the Protestant oligarchs in the city, albeit only after a protracted campaign for civil rights and electoral reform, reflected their successes in the business life of the city, especially in the butter trade and the tanning, brewing and distilling industries. Those successes were also reflected in the ostentatious building of Catholic churches once the Penal Laws were repealed. The Cathedral of St Mary and St Anne was built on the brow of the hill at Shandon from 1808, a massive monument to the religious commitment, but also the sheer confidence, of Cork's Catholic community at the start of the nineteenth century. Holy Trinity Church on Fr Mathew's Quay, a marvellous neo-Gothic building, was built between 1825 and 1832. St Patrick's church on the Lower Glanmire Road, an impressive building in the classical style, was opened in 1836. St Mary's church on Pope's Quay, a beautiful building in the classical style that was designed gratis by a local Protestant architect named Kearns Deane, was built between 1832 and 1839.

Carty's map of Cork in 1726 shows the expansion of Cork's suburbs north and south of the Lee, and also the significant progress being made in extending the city centre eastwards around Paul Street and George's Street (now Oliver Plunkett Street).

Crawford Art Gallery on Emmet Place in Cork used to be the Customs House, and ships berthed where citizens now frequent an outdoor market. (Courtesy of John Mullins.)

Robert Walker's sketch of Butt's panoramic view of Cork in 1760. Note Shandon's steeple on the right, the Customs House in the centre and on the left, Merchants Quay, with a drawbridge across the river channel that would later form Patrick's Street.

By the time that William IV's reign came to an end in 1837, Cork's Catholic middle classes were able to point to significant progress made by their community in business and in the professions, in education and in society at large. Residual discrimination against Catholics would continue to be a feature of the upper eschelons of life in Cork right up until independence, and it left a residue of resentment that persisted in blighting relations between Cork's Catholics and Protestants in the early twentieth century.

PHYSICAL EXPANSION

As Cork's economy and population grew, so too did its physical extent. John Carty's map of Cork in 1726 showed that the northern suburbs had by then extended as far north as Blackpool. On the south side there was expansion along the Bandon Road and at Gallows Green, but this part of the city was far less developed than was the northern suburb. Most strikingly, Carty's map reflects remarkable progress made in reclaiming the marshes of the Lee. The channel separating the two central islands of the Lee had been arched over in 1705. The north-east marsh around Paul Street was joined to the medieval city at Daunt's Square. Bridges from Daunt's Square and Tuckey Street linked Dunscombe's marsh to the medieval city, and there were many buildings between George's Street (now Oliver Plunkett Street) and the river channel that would one day become Patrick's Street. The South Mall was being built up, though there was still a river channel separating it from Morrison's Island. Carty's map also shows the Mardyke embankment, which was built in 1719.

In 1750, there was still a river channel where Patrick's Street would be created, but it was crossed by a drawbridge from Drawbridge Street to the vicinity of today's Merchants Quay. Development along George's Street on Dunscombe's marsh continued apace. Pike's marsh, west of the river channel which later formed Grattan Street, was built up, while nearby Hammond's marsh boasted a 'large pleasant bowling green planted on its margins with trees, kept regularly cut, whose shade makes it an agreeable walk … and on it a band of musicians has been supported by subscription for the entertainment of the gentlemen and ladies who frequent it'. Beside the bowling green stood an Assembly House wherein 'assemblies are held two days in the week, and also a weekly concert'.

Charles Smith's 'View of Cork' and John Butt's painting of the city show how Cork had expanded greatly beyond its medieval walls. In fact, the walls were demolished in many places by then, and by 1800 almost none of them were left standing above ground level. Smith noted that the medieval Main Street was 'intermixed with old and new buildings, and as the former decay new ones rise in modern taste'. Contemporary images show many Dutch-style buildings along the city's northern quays. Arthur Young, writing in the 1770s, observed that Cork resembled a Dutch town 'for there are many canals in the streets with quays before the houses'.

Yet, as time went by, more and more of Cork's river channels were arched over or filled in. Rocque's map of Cork in 1773 shows most of Cornmarket Street had been laid out. George's Quay was in place and streets were being laid out towards Douglas Street and along the South Terrace towards Infirmary Road. Henry Street was arched over in 1774. Grattan Street followed in 1778, the Grand Parade in 1780 and Patrick's Street in 1783.

Vehicular access to the islands of the Lee was only possible by way of the North Gate Bridge and the South Gate Bridge until the mid-eighteenth century. However, from 1761 the corporation set about building a bridge from Prince's Street to Morrison's Island,

Above left: The river channel that subsequently became Patrick's Street around the statue, shown in Walker's version of Butt's view of Cork.

Above right: Patrick Street is curved in line with the river channel that used to separate the north-east marsh from Dunscombe's marsh until late in Georgian times. (Courtesy of John Mullins.)

Clarke's Bridge, built in 1776, is one of the oldest surviving bridges in Cork.

and another connecting the island to Red Abbey marsh. The latter
bridge was replaced by Parliament Bridge in 1806. Clarke's Bridge,
linking Hanover Street to the southern suburbs, was built in 1776. In
1763, the corporation debated whether to build a drawbridge where
Patrick's Bridge now stands. Most councillors at the time, however,
feared that a bridge there would make the extensive quays as far as
the North Gate Bridge redundant. The problems of congestion on
the North Gate Bridge had to grow a great deal worse, and opposition from ferrymen and other concerned citizens overcome, before
finally, on 25 July 1788, the foundation stone of Patrick's Bridge was
laid. The bridge was completed in September 1789.

Beauford's map of Cork in 1801 is readily recognisable. The main
thoroughfares, the North and South Main Streets, Patrick's Street,
Grand Parade, George's Street, and the many lesser streets joined to
them were in place, and the South Mall would be filled in in 1801-2.
A grand central business district was emerging in Cork's new wide
streets to the east of the medieval core of Cork. A Persian visitor to
Cork in 1799 remarked that Cork's shops were 'handsome and filled
with every requisite, either for use or luxury'.

Beauford's map of Cork in 1801. Note the Navigation Wall built downstream of the city towards Blackrock to improve shipping access to the city quays.

The medieval lanes of Cork were being abandoned to the poor, at high rents. A report of 1804 stated that in the lanes 'every apartment from the cellar to the garret is crowded by tenants labouring under the complicated calamities of disease and poverty'. John Carr, writing in 1805, observed that in many lanes there were small wretched dwellings with upwards of fifty people. A visitor to Cork complained of the, 'muddy and ill-paved streets … Rain, noise, filth, drunkenness and distress are in every street, and the beggars are a perpetual source of misery'.

The South Gate Bridge around 1770. Notice the people searching for shellfish in the Lee. This area would be redeveloped by the Wide Street Commissioners in the early nineteenth century. (Courtesy of Cork City Libraries.)

The North Mall. Wealthy citizens in Georgian Cork were keen to put distance between themselves and slum dwellers. (Courtesy of Cork City Libraries.)

The middle classes were removing themselves from the worst of such filth and distress over the course of the second half of the eighteenth century. To the west of Grattan Street and along the North Mall, many attractive houses were built. This area was crowned with Cork's Mansion House looking westwards over the Mardyke meadows. The mansion was the mayor's official residence and a centre of social intercourse for Cork's Protestant elite. Many merchants and professional families moved into houses, or into apartments above commercial premises, on the Grand Parade and along the other new streets on the east of the city. The most wealthy began to leave the city altogether. Horatio Townshend, writing in a book published by the Royal Dublin Society in 1810, noted that since the completion of Patrick's Bridge, many excellent houses were built on the north side of the river, towards Montenotte, 'which has lately become one of the most fashionable places of residence'. Around that same time John Carr was impressed to see 'so many handsome houses, some of them owned by rich Catholic merchants'.

Great George's Street (Washington Street) was developed to form a new 'western entrance' to the city. It was designed by George and James Pain and was inspired by Regent Street in London. Windele remarked that:

> ... this street is by far the most regular, as it is the newest of all our streets, the houses are built with uniformity, possess good shops and have altogether a pleasing effect and appearance, but it is still incomplete. The site of this beautiful street a few years ago was occupied by some of the narrowest and filthiest lanes and alleys of the old town and was densely inhabited by a squalid and impoverished population.

In 1835, Robert Graham, a Scotsman, visited Cork and left an account of his impressions. He thought Cork was 'more distinguished than almost any town I have been in'. He thought the South Mall 'very handsome' but the city's main thoroughfare, Patrick's Street, struck him as 'the handsomest street, and one not easily to be matched in many places'. He was impressed by the size and elegance of the city's new Custom House, built in 1818, which reflected the fact that Cork was 'a town of considerable trade'. The new courthouse on Great George's Street struck him as the city's 'greatest architectural ornament'. He noted too that the Catholics were, 'doing a great deal in the way of building and improving their chapels'. I must also mention Blackrock Castle, which was rebuilt anew in 1829, after a fire destroyed its predecessor, to provide a graceful architectural setting for Cork corporation's banquets and other convivial gatherings. It was no longer true, as it was at the start of the nineteenth century, that Cork lacked public buildings of interest.

CONCLUSION

Cork was completely transformed over the course of Georgian times. At the start of the eighteenth century the city was spreading into the suburbs north and south of the Lee but it was still recognisable as the medieval walled town it used to be. By the early nineteenth century the medieval walls had virtually disappeared. The city had expanded greatly across the islands of the Lee and its centre of gravity had been shifted decisively to Patrick Street, where it has since remained. Its economy had grown many times over, with food processing, brewing and distilling, and a large textiles industry forming the main bases for its wealth and employment, along with the large services sectors in retailing and the provision of professional services to an extensive hinterland in southern Ireland. The busy entrepreneurs of the Protestant oligarchs in eighteenth-century Cork showed no interest in preserving the city's medieval past, neither its walls nor churches nor other public buildings. They built a new, Georgian city on top of the old. However, with the rise of the Catholic middle class in later Georgian times, there was a greater interest in architecture in the city. A number of impressive Catholic churches were built to symbolise the emergence of a new elite in Cork. New public buildings of architectural note were constructed around the same time, and piece by piece the city that we recognise today was emerging.

Many people in Cork were troubled by poverty, overcrowded housing, insanitary and unhygienic living conditions, the smells and sicknesses caused by human and animal waste on the streets and lanes everywhere and the by-products of the meat processing yards off Blarney Street. Nonetheless, Corkonians were conscious of the fact that theirs was a great and important city, and they looked forward to what still promised to be a brighter future.

8

VICTORIAN TIMES

Queen Victoria visited Cork in 1849, and was presented with a salmon by the fishermen at Blackrock. A shopping emporium in the city was renamed the Queen's Old Castle in her honour. The Cove of Cork (Cóbh) was renamed Queenstown. Victoria's reign witnessed the construction of some of Cork's most striking and beloved public buildings, including the Queen's College and St Fin Barre's Cathedral. Streets and quays, a city park and a hospital were named in her honour or that of her husband, Albert. Her reign was the age of the steam train, and later of the electric tram. It was a time when more and more people recognised education as a means to a better future. Late Victorian times witnessed a tremendous improvement in the quality of most people's lives in Cork, and in the physical environment of the city. Nonetheless, the elegant facades of many public buildings and homes in Cork belied the reality of economic difficulties in the city, and poverty which blighted countless lives.

ECONOMY

All of the main industries that experienced growth in Cork in Georgian times declined thereafter. This is starkly reflected in the fact that while 40 per cent of male workers in the city were employed in manufacturing in 1841, by 1901 the figure had fallen to 19 per cent. The reasons for the decline of Cork's industries are not yet clear. Some historians have suggested that there was a failure of enterprise in Cork, and/or a failure to keep abreast of developing technologies. However, Cork's experience reflects a broader pattern, not just across most of Ireland beyond Belfast, but across most of Europe. Industrial development across nineteenth-century Europe was very strongly associated with coalfields. Economic historians may argue that distance from sources of coal should not have been an obstacle to industrial growth, but in practice it was.

The textile industry in Cork had grown around fast-flowing rivers, like the Bride and Glen that fed into the Lee. However, water power in Cork's hinterland had limited potential for development, and the costs of converting textile plants from water power to coal, and the on-going costs of importing coal from south Wales and transporting it in quantity from the port of Cork inland, were usually prohibitively expensive. Once the commercial terms of the Act of Union came into force in 1824, Cork's textile businesses collapsed in the face of overwhelming competition from English plants. Cork's woollen industry alone had exported up to 300,000 yards of woollen yarn per annum at the start of the nineteenth century, yet by 1830 its export trade had all but disappeared. Cork's linen and cotton industries disappeared. That extraordinary decline in the textile industry caused massive unemployment in Cork, and a huge fall in the wages paid to those still employed in the sector. According to Angela Fahy, wage rates for weavers fell by as much as 80 per cent between 1820 and 1850.

Developments such as the introduction of the sewing machine, on the other hand, created new business opportunities and facilitated the establishment of a successful shirt-making industry in the city. According to Louis Cullen, Arnottes employed 1,000 people in Cork in 1850 in the manufacturing of silk ties and shirts. Mahony's of Blarney employed 200 people working in the local woollen mills there. A feature common to all of the textile enterprises was the predominance of women and children employed in order to minimise wage costs.

The glass industry in Cork, which in 1835 employed 250 people, fell victim to cheaper English imports by 1846. Shipbuilding too, which was a major industry in Cork from 1815, declined sharply. The costs of accessing coal and iron and steel put it at a great disadvantage compared with English shipbuilders. In addition, the river channel to Cork was very shallow at low tide and that created great difficulties at a time when average vessel sizes were increasing. It was not until the late nineteenth century that the channel was dredged sufficiently to allow large ships to reach the city's lower quays. As shipbuilding declined in Cork, and as steam replaced wind in powering ships, the sail-cloth industry in Douglas declined towards extinction. There were still opportunities for rope-makers in Victorian times, though. There were seven rope-works in Cork in 1880, but thereafter the industry was consolidated into two larger, more mechanised plants with fewer employees.

The provisions trade, the mainstay of Cork's economy in the eighteenth century, declined in the nineteenth century. The Butter Exchange at Shandon, erected in 1849, still serves as a testament to the great wealth that the butter trade once brought to the city. However, Cork's most distant export markets in the Americas, India and Australasia were progressively lost to competitors who were better placed in the United States and Australia. Butter exports to mainland Europe declined too, as different countries sought to become self-sufficient. The loss of distant markets obliged Cork's butter merchants to depend increasingly on the nearby British market. As late as 1870, 30 per cent of Ireland's butter exports were shipped from Cork.

Between 1871 and 1875, British imports of cheap butter substitutes from mainland Europe almost doubled, and imports of Cork butter plummeted. Cork butter also lost market share in Britain to butter imports from mainland Europe. The very high salt content of Cork butter fell out of favour with consumers, and quality controls failed to keep abreast of consumers' rising expectations. It was not until 1891 that special compartments were introduced for the storage of butter on ships to Britain, but by that time the reputation of Cork butter had suffered irreparable harm. Between 1877 and 1891, butter exports from Cork fell by about 60 per cent. Cork's once-mighty butter trade was in terminal decline.

Cork's Butter Exchange at Shandon. (Courtesy of Cork City Libraries.)

Cork's other provisions trades also declined sharply. By 1853, the barrelled-meat provisions trade had been virtually wiped out due to competition in distant markets, and a shift to fresh meat consumption closer to home. On the other hand, the advent of the steamship facilitated the increased export of livestock; in 1849 some 201,181 cattle were exported live from Cork. Pig meat was a growth area in the late nineteenth century, with a market for salted and smoked bacon, and the later development of refrigeration. Lunham's in Cork slaughtered 30,000 pigs in 1878, a number that increased to 127,000 in 1881.

The overall decline in Cork's provisions trade had knock-on effects amongst related industries, and especially for the coopers who used to make the barrels in which the salted provisions had been stored, and the salters who cured the food. The number of tanneries fell also, as fewer cattle were slaughtered in Cork, from sixty tanning yards in 1845 to sixteen in 1853. Other industries that depended on the by-products of meat processing, such as candle-making and shoemaking, also declined greatly. Towards the end of the nineteenth century there was a number of boot factories established in Cork, starting with the Cork Boot Factory in Blackpool. These factories were highly mechanised and tapped into a growing domestic market as living standards improved. The Lee Boot Factory opened in new premises on Great George's Street (now Washington Street) in 1885, and continued in operation until the 1980s.

Cork's grain trade was considerable in the first half of the nineteenth century, buoyed by the protective Corn Laws. In 1833, Cork exported 126,519 barrels of oats, 72,654 barrels of wheat and 1,749 barrels of barley (barley being required locally for brewing and distilling). A new Cornmarket was built to cater for the expanding export market in that year. However, the abolition of the Corn Laws during the famine led to the virtual collapse of the grain trade in Cork in the face of American competition. The Cornmarket, like the Butter Exchange, became another reminder of bygone days.

Brewing and distilling, which were major employers early in the nineteenth century, were hard hit by Fr Theobald Mathew's temperance movement, which aimed to improve the lives of the poor. The movement was founded in Cork in 1838 and by January 1839 200,000 people had been enrolled. While the benefits it brought to its members and their families are not to be doubted, it led to a dramatic slump in alcohol consumption in Cork, the closure of many public houses and a significant fall in production in both the breweries and distilleries. Whiskey consumption was hardest hit by the temperance movement. There was some recovery in brewing and distilling over the course of the second half of the nineteenth century. In 1856, Murphy's Brewery at Lady's Well began to produce stout and porter. Its porter became a local favourite, and by 1890 Murphy's was Cork's leading brewery. Lady's Well is now the last brewery still in business in Cork, albeit as part of the Dutch brewing giant Heineken.

In an effort to rebuild Cork's industrial base after the Great Famine, an industrial exhibition was organised by Sir George Benson on Anglesea Street in 1853. It was attended by 138,375 people over the three months it was held. After the exhibition the building was used as a Corn Exchange, and later it became Cork's City Hall. The exhibition succeeded in generating publicity for Cork's business enterprises, and in injecting some short-term confidence, but no exhibition could make Cork a major industrial centre in the late nineteenth century.

Instead, Cork consolidated its role as the retail and services centre of Munster. It was a role the city held before the famine, but the building of the extensive Great Southern & Western Railway network, and the smaller networks joining the city by rail to Passage West, Bandon and the south coast, Macroom and Muskerry, greatly strengthened its market position in the second half of the nineteenth century, as income levels rose beyond subsistence level for more and more of the population. Patrick's Street boasted great emporia to attract the discerning customer with cash to spend on luxury goods. The South Mall boasted the services of law firms and accountants, a range of banks and other commercial services. The port of Cork exported far less than it had done in Georgian times, but its quays were busy enough with imports of consumer goods in demand in the city and across the province of Munster. There was money to be made in Cork but, like any other Victorian city, there was a great gap between the incomes enjoyed by the wealthy few and the many poor.

Cork, over the course of Victorian times, suffered from 'de-industrialisation'. The decline of the provisions trade was probably inevitable, as other states became more self-sufficient and/or developed their own export trades, particularly the United States. Yet there seems to have been some failure of enterprise in the city to develop new business opportunities. Cork's peripheral location in relation to sources of coal, when the industrial revolution in Victorian times was based on steam power, as well as external markets, left Cork disadvantaged compared to the major industrial complexes which grew up on Britain's coalfields. Only in food processing, in which Cork enjoyed comparative advantages, were there any great profits made in the second half of the nineteenth century.

THE FAMINE

When William Thackeray visited Cork in 1841 he was disgusted by the number of beggars he encountered in alleys 'where the odours and rags and the darkness are so hideous that one runs frightened away from them'. Two years earlier, a workhouse for the poor of Cork had been established off the Douglas Road, on the site of today's St Finbarr's Hospital, but the poor were actively discouraged from venturing within its ominous walls. No one was prepared for a catastrophic famine.

County Cork escaped the worst effects of the infamous potato blight when it arrived in Ireland in 1845, but in 1846 the blight struck in earnest. Fr Mathew wrote of seeing countless people 'wringing their hands and wailing bitterly [at] the destruction that had left them foodless'. Starving wretches began to flood into Cork in desperate hope of finding food. Dr Callanan, one of Cork's workhouse doctors, wrote that, 'one third of the daily population of our streets consisted of shadows and spectres, the impersonations of disease and famine, crowding in from the rural districts to the general doom – the grave ...'.

A contemporary image of starvation in the Great Famine: Brigid O'Donnell and her two children.

However, not all of the victims of the famine came from the countryside. As rural incomes declined sharply, so did the market for goods and services provided in Cork. In 1847, it was reported that 1,000 of Cork's tradesmen were unemployed. In Blackrock about a quarter of the workforce was unemployed. Back then, if the working classes didn't work, they didn't have money to eat. Hunger and disease became rampant among the poor city dwellers.

In October 1846, there were ten Relief Committee depots in Cork, feeding 25,000 people. Sometimes it was necessary to call on the police to keep order among the starving masses. The St Vincent de Paul Society provided much-needed charity, as did the Quaker community in the city. The starving and the sick besieged the workhouse on the Douglas Road. To relieve pressure, 500 beggars were admitted to the workhouse in one week alone. By the end of January 1847 there were 5,309 inmates in the workhouse – far more than the number it was designed to accommodate. Typhus and relapsing fevers spread like wildfire among the malnourished masses crowded in insanitary conditions. On 29 March 1847, after 757 inmates died in the workhouse in that month alone, the decision was taken to close the institution until conditions improved. The workhouse, auxiliary workhouses and the fever hospitals simply could not cope with the deluge of misery heaped upon them. A *cordon sanitaire* was put in place around the city to stem the flood of sick people arriving from the countryside. The city graveyards were literally filled with bodies. At the start of June 1847, St Joseph's cemetery was closed to any more burials and corpses were sent to Curraghkippane cemetery north of Cork and to a famine graveyard on Carr's Hill off the road to Carrigaline.

A famine soup kitchen operated by Cork's Quaker community.

About 72,000 people emigrated from Cork between 1845 and 1851. Cork's county population fell by a quarter due to death and emigration. However, the city's population grew, from 80,720 in 1841 to 85,745, because the number of country people who moved to the city more than made up for the numbers of Corkonians who died or left. The famine was officially declared over in August 1847, but the economic dislocation and the psychological scars took many more years to come to terms with.

RAILWAYS

The Great Southern & Western Railway Company was incorporated in 1844 to build a railway line from Dublin to Cork, a distance of 165 miles, making it the longest railway line in Ireland or Britain at that time. On 29 October 1849, the first train to Cork arrived at Blackpool, on the city's northside. It was a tremendous achievement. Six years later the track was extended to a terminus at Penrose Quay by means of a 1,355-yard tunnel. In 1866, the GS & WR purchased the Cork & Youghal Railway Company, and ran its trains through to Youghal and Queenstown.

In 1846, the Cork, Blackrock & Passage Railway Company was incorporated, and its train services commenced on 8 June 1850, between its terminus at Albert Street in Cork and the quays at Passage West. The CB & PR also ran a fleet of steamships from Patrick's Bridge to Passage, and later to Glenbrook, Monkstown, Ringaskiddy, Hawlbowline, Queenstown and Aghada. Its railway track ran alongside the Marina for part of its journey.

The Marina, one of Cork's most beautiful promenades, was begun in 1763 as a navigation wall designed to help scour the main channel of the River Lee from Blackrock to the city quays from the shoals of mud that clogged it at low tide. From the mid-nineteenth century, mud dredged from the Lee was used to reclaim the slobland behind the Marina. Cork's corporation had hoped to sell the land to private developers, but it did not attract industrial investors until Henry Ford established his car-manufacturing plant there in 1917. In the meantime, the 230 acres of former slobland became Victoria Park, an impressive amenity area which was officially opened in 1854. The Marina was adorned with a double row of elm trees planted by Prof. Thomas Murphy of Queen's College, Cork. The train services of the Cork, Blackrock & Passage Railway company were extended to Monkstown, Carrigaline and Crosshaven between 1902 and 1904.

The Cork & Bandon Railway Company was incorporated in 1846. Its railway track was constructed in stages from Bandon, reaching Albert Quay in Cork on 1 December 1851. In 1888, having amalgamated with several smaller companies, it became the Cork, Bandon & South Coast Railway Company and joined Cork to Bantry, Clonakilty and Baltimore. The Cork & Macroom Direct Railway joined that town in mid-west County Cork to Albert Quay in 1866. It opened its own terminus in Cork at Capwell in 1879. The Cork and Muskerry Light Railway ran from Bishop's Marsh, an island on the River Lee off the Western Road, to Blarney from 1887, to Coachford in 1888 and Donoughmore in 1893.

The first train on the Cork, Blackrock and Passage Railway line, near Blackrock, in June 1850.

CMLR train on the Western Road heading towards Muskerry. (Photographed by H.C. Casserley in 1932.)

Cork's railways carried passengers and freight, and tied the countryside ever more firmly to the city. Trains brought butter to the city and livestock to its markets or quays. They also brought customers from the countryside to Cork's shops and other businesses. In the other direction, the railways carried goods made in Cork or, in larger volume, goods imported from England via Cork, such as clothes, furniture, books, and the other trappings of British Victorian society. Railways facilitated a cultural revolution that modernised Irish society and made it seem that the Irish would be fully assimilated into British society. In one respect, though, the railways brought surprisingly little change to Cork. No suburbs grew up around any of the railway stations outside the city, not even at Blackrock. Why that was is unclear, though I suspect that the locations of the railway termini were generally inconvenient for the city centre. A horse-drawn tram network was opened in 1872 to join the termini of the Dublin, Bandon and Passage railway lines with each other and Patrick Street, but it closed after only three years of costly failure.

In 1898, the Cork Electric Lighting and Tramway Company opened for business. As its name indicates it generated electricity for street lighting, but also for domestic use. It operated no fewer than thirty-five electric tramcars from its depot by Albert Road to serve three cross-city routes: Douglas to Blackpool, Blackrock to Tivoli, and Summerhill to Sunday's Well. The regular and reliable service encouraged suburbanisation along the main roads to Douglas, Blackrock, Summerhill and Tivoli. Though the electric trams trundled around the streets of Cork for only thirty-one years in all, they have left an indelible impression on the popular image of Cork in days of yore.

SOCIETY

The 1861 census revealed that 84 per cent of the population of Cork were Catholics. However, almost half of the employers in the city, and a very high proportion of the professional classes and skilled manual workers, were Protestants. Though the Catholic business elite in the city enjoyed a great deal of advancement in Victorian times, they were still outranked socially by their Protestant counterparts. One reflection of the Protestant sense of superiority that continued to rankle Catholic

Guy's map of Cork in 1893 shows the railway lines into Cork's termini at Penrose Quay, Albert Street, Albert Quay, Capwell and Western Road. The shaded area represents the medieval walled city. (Courtesy of Cork City Libraries.)

sensitivities was that the Royal Cork Yacht Club was so exclusive that the rich city merchants were obliged to form their own Munster Model Yacht Club in 1872. Nonetheless, over the course of Victorian times, and even by 1881, Catholics achieved a dominant position in the professions and more proportionate shares of senior positions in business and in the public service. This reflected the greater opportunities opened up by the emergence of a 'meritocracy' among people with education across the United Kingdom. Nonetheless, the building of a great Church of Ireland Cathedral in Cork from 1865 was intended to remind everybody that the Anglo-Irish, as many of the Protestant ascendancy considered themselves to be, were 'no mean people'.

On the other hand, poorer Protestants in Cork were reduced in number, partly through emigration to places of better opportunity elsewhere in the British empire, but also due to assimilation with their working-class Catholic neighbours. The clearances of the city centre slums in the early twentieth century saw a strikingly high proportion of people with English surnames rehoused in the northside of Cork.

It was noted in the previous chapter that from the late eighteenth century, Cork's merchants had been leaving the city to reside in large villas overlooking the Lee at Montenotte. However, the professional classes still resided in the city centre before the Great Famine. Windele remarked in 1839 that the reclaimed eastern part of the city was inhabited primarily by professional people living above their businesses premises, or in close proximity to them. In 1845, only thirteen of the ninety-eight lawyers in Cork had separate addresses for their workplace and residence. By 1863, more than half the number of lawyers had separate addresses. It is possible that the awful conditions

The neo-Gothic Cathedral of St Fin Barre is my favourite building in Cork. Construction started in 1865 and in 1870 the unfinished building was consecrated. The spires were completed in 1879. William Burges, its architect, gave the church a gold resurrection angel, which stands on the pinnacle of the sanctuary roof.

in Cork during the famine accelerated a trend towards suburbanisation in the city. Even the formerly 'wealthy streets' around Cork's
Mansion House (subsequently the Mercy Hospital) such as Millerd
Street, Moore Street, Devonshire Street and Peter Street had lost their
'grandeur and gentility' by the mid-nineteenth century.

The medieval core of Cork City, and most of the inner suburbs
at Barrack Street and Shandon, were increasingly abandoned to the
poor. The back lanes off the North and South Main Streets were
packed with overcrowded tenements. The main thoroughfares outside of the new city centre still tended to house shopkeepers and
publicans above their businesses. Windele described Barrack Street as
'unsavouring of antiquity, strongly marked by neglect, age and decay,
but teaming with population and presenting all the characters of an
Irish suburb in general'. He described the Ballymacthomas area on
the northside as an 'extremely populated suburb … the ramifications
are extremely minute and the ways and passages rather labyrinthine.
Tanneries and slaughter houses located here give a rather sombre
appearance'. There were extensive 'cabin suburbs' around Blackpool
and Glasheen, both former centres of the textiles industry. These were
made up of very small one- or two-room cabins crowded together.

There were few houses to the west of Cork. As late as 1860, according
to Gibson, 'the tide of population and hum of business did not extend
west of Grattan Street'. The Mardyke was antiquated and had lost its
former status as a recreational area. Large public institutions tended to
be built west of the city: the city and county gaols on opposite banks of
the Lee, the Queen's College (opened in 1849) and the lunatic asylum
(the largest in Ireland, opened in 1847). An exception to that pattern was
the construction of the Cork Workhouse off the Douglas Road in 1839.

As Cork's economy experienced deindustrialisation, it was the
labouring classes who suffered the most. Wage rates fell as unemployment rose. For example, in 1821 Cork coopers' wages were set at 20
shillings per week, but by the 1840s they had fallen to between 7 and
10 shillings per week. Employers turned increasingly to casual labourers, and women and children, to cut their wage costs. Mechanisation
and improved forms of mass production were greatly feared by
skilled workers, as their places could be taken by machinery operated by unskilled, and therefore cheaper, workers. In the 1870s, for
example, the Cork Steam Packet Company's steam-powered sawmill
was operated by a single sawyer, helped by seven unskilled labourers.

Cork's skilled workers formed trade unions in later Victorian times to protect their interests. The City of Cork Coopers' Benevolent Society was established in 1886. However, as late as 1900, while 70 per cent of Cork's skilled workers were members of a union, as few as 30 per cent of unskilled workers were unionised.

Within the labour movement there was a republican element, and nationalism and labour grievances were intermeshed to a degree. In 1865, there were 4,000 Fenian members in Cork, which was, in fact, double the number of union members. However, nationalist sentiment in Cork did not prevent many young Corkmen from poor backgrounds from enlisting in the British army during the Boer War or the first half of the Great War. Maura Cronin has observed that 'it is difficult to identify any clear strand of working class consciousness in nineteenth century Cork'. She pointed out that Cork's trade unions were socially conservative, perhaps because of the influence of the Catholic Church but also because of 'the skilled worker's sharp contempt for the unskilled and his fear that the gap between the two groups might be narrowed by radical political activity'. On the other hand, divisions among workers could be bridged by common allegiance to sports clubs and musical bands. Cronin concluded that, 'Cork was a classical Victorian city with a prosperous commercial elite, aspiring retailing sector and impoverished lower class. Inter-group division, shaped by religion, access to wealth and occupation, was bridged by the relative smallness of the city but progressively widened as suburban expansion accompanied city-centre stagnation.'

Margaret Place near Cove Street. Many poor families in Cork lived in such neighbourhoods in Victorian times. (Courtesy of Cork City Libraries.)

PUBLIC HEALTH

Victoria's reign was an age of improvement in many respects, not least of them the provision of public health amenities. Of course, much of that improvement was in response to the high death rates experienced during epidemics of cholera and other deadly diseases. In 1847, the Improvements Clauses Act empowered Cork Corporation to remove and demolish dangerous buildings, to clean the streets, develop drainage, lighting and generally improve the environment in the city. Plans for public buildings had to be approved, slaughter houses had to be licensed, and provision had to be made for public open spaces and public recreation. More rigorous housing standards were enforced, streets were paved and kept clean, and sewers were constructed.

In 1856, Cork Corporation was authorised by an Act of parliament to take control of the Pipe Water Company and to provide clean water to the population within a three-mile radius of the General Post Office on George's Street (Oliver Plunkett Street). Cast-iron pipes were laid down, the reservoirs were expanded and public health in the city was improved. Nonetheless, more had to be done. In 1871, there was a smallpox outbreak within the city. Dr MacNaughton Jones reported that, 'one third of the cases in my district, and a large portion of deaths, occurred in a small circle' around Ballymacthomas. He ascribed the outbreak to unhygienic living conditions, since Sunday's Well, another part of his district, had few cases. Outbreaks of enteric fever in 1877, and typhus in 1881, 1884, 1886 and 1891 resulted in a total of 3,351 cases reported in the city, of which 189 people died. Between 1891 and 1900 there was an annual average of 290 deaths in Cork from tuberculosis.

The corporation was forced to address the problem of slum housing in the city. In the late 1870s, over 100 houses in districts prone to cholera, smallpox and typhus epidemics, around Evergreen Road, the North Main Street and the Watercourse Road were cleared and the land was redeveloped by the Improved Dwellings Company, a profit-making philanthropic organisation. The corporation itself began to build series of workmen's cottages, starting with Madden's Buildings (1886), Ryan's Buildings (1888), Horgan's Buildings (1891) and Roche's Buildings the following year. In 1903, Barrett's Buildings were built, followed in 1906 by Kelleher's and Sutton's Buildings. The new cottages typically consisted of three rooms – two bedrooms and a living room. They were built on the outskirts of the city on the advice of the city's medical officer of health, who argued that no building should be allowed on the flat of the city as that would be 'perpetuating slums'. Instead, he advised the corporation to build cottages in 'pure and open air and on virgin soil'.

The scale of rehousing in late Victorian times was modest in relation to the problem being addressed because of insufficient finance, but a significant start in the provision of public housing had been made. The death rate fell significantly as a result of the public health initiatives undertaken in the city. In 1877, the death rate in Cork reached the staggering scale of 152 per 1,000 births. By 1910 it had fallen below 100 deaths per 1,000 births.

EDUCATION

In Victorian times, education was recognised as a critical means of social and personal advancement. In 1831, the national school system was established and offered virtually free education to all. In 1835, Dr Murphy, Catholic bishop of Cork, revealed that 5,000 children were being educated under his supervision. In 1841, 47 per cent of people aged five and over were literate. By 1911, no fewer than 88 per cent were literate. Literacy improved people's life chances tremendously and had an enormous impact on popular culture in Cork. Many Corkonians, to the later laments of Gaelic Leaguers, enjoyed reading Dickens, Thackeray and Hardy and other illuminati of Victorian England's renaissance in print. Indeed, Cork was a city with an impressive array of bookshops into the 1980s, with the Lee Book Store in particular being a treasure trove of literary Victoriana.

Post-primary education was still the preserve of a privileged minority of children before the 1960s. Nonetheless, the Church of Ireland maintained a grammar school until 1885, when it was brought under the control of the Cork City School Board. Rochelle Seminary was established to provide an education for Protestant girls. The burgeoning of post-primary education for Catholics dated from the establishment of the Ursuline Convent in Blackrock in 1771, and involved an array of religious orders; including most prominently the Presentation Sisters, Sisters of Mercy, Presentation Brothers, and

Christian Brothers. The orders moulded the young minds entrusted to them in a decidedly conservative, Catholic and nationalist manner. Their influence on society in Cork in the late nineteenth and twentieth centuries is simply incalculable.

Queen's College, Cork, was founded in 1845 and opened its doors to university students in 1849. Its history has been told in detail by John A. Murphy, and will simply be sketched here. Cork's was one of three new colleges established in Ireland (the others being at Belfast and Galway) to make universities accessible to the rising professional and commercial classes. There had already been a strong demand for a university college to be set up in the city. However, the Catholic Church strongly disapproved of what it termed the 'godless' colleges, because of their non-denominational character, and its opposition stunted their development at Cork and Galway.

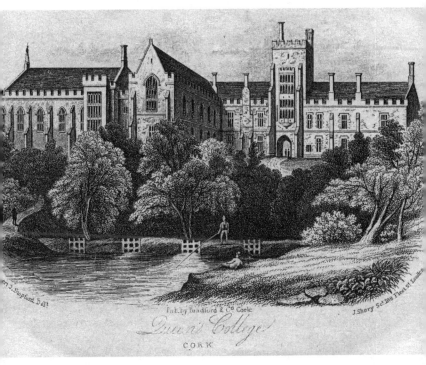

Queen's College, Cork, as it appeared from the Western Road.

Queen's College, Cork, was built on top of a limestone escarpment overlooking the River Lee, a site which its architect, Sir Thomas Deane, described as, 'excellent and commanding and most beautiful for a public building'. Deane's neo-Gothic design impressed everyone, and inspired Macaulay's observation that the college was 'worthy to stand in the High Street of Oxford'. As John A. Murphy has written, the quadrangle 'remains to this day a place of soft brightness and tranquillity and, in sunshine, of basking warmth'. For graduates of the college, a stroll around the quadrangle still conjures up happy memories of student days.

One hundred and twelve students attended the college from its official opening in 1849. The courses available to them, in law, medicine and arts, including science, agriculture and engineering, reflected the philosophy of the college's first president, Robert Kane, who believed in higher education being 'useful knowledge'. He promised that the college would 'educate young men for the active age and world in which we live'. At the same time, he associated the institution with Cork's patron saint. The college's motto is, 'Where Finbarr taught let Munster learn'. Unfortunately, the intransigence of the Catholic bishops stifled much of the college's potential as an institution that might have supported the economic development of the Cork region.

Nonetheless, Queen's College, Cork, grew slowly for a time, with 300 students in 1879/80. The first female students joined the college in 1885/86. They were welcomed by the college president of the day, William K. Sullivan, who expressed the hope that 'their example will stimulate the men to more attentive and regular work'. The appointment of Mary Ryan as professor of Romance Languages in 1910 made her the first woman in the United Kingdom of Great Britain and Ireland to hold a chair. By 1913/14 there were 76 women among the 430 students at the college. Since the late 1980s, female students outnumber males.

A new era in the history of the college dawned with the Irish Universities Act (1908), which transformed it into University College Cork, a constituent of the National University of Ireland. Under Sir Bertram Windele, characterised by John A. Murphy as one of the outstanding presidents in the history of the college, UCC 'entered the second phase of its history, with a new name, new charter and a greatly extended range of departments … This was a revolutionary expansion of academic disciplines that confidently invited a corresponding growth in student numbers.' With the heavy hand of the Catholic Church finally lifted, UCC was finally free to realise its potential.

CONCLUSION

Queen Victoria died in 1901. By then Cork's population stood at 76,122, only very slightly more than a decade earlier. The city centre and the older suburbs would be readily recognisable today. Its streets, river channels, most of its bridges, virtually all of the central city churches and other public buildings were in place. The electric street lights, the electric tramcars and the trains, not to mention the occasional car, gave the city a comfortably modern feel and a dynamism which helped to disguise the limited industrial growth it enjoyed in the reign of Victoria.

Patrick Street in 1900.

We are all reasonably familiar with black and white photographs of Cork from the turn of the twentieth century. Remarkably, though, we can now see Cork and its people alive at the very start of the twentieth century through the films of Sagar Mitchell and James Kenyon, who ran a cinematograph company from Blackburn in the north of England. Their films of Cork, especially that of a 'Tram ride from King's Street to Patrick's Bridge' and the 'Views from the Grand Parade', offer fascinating, if poignant, impressions of our ancestors; men, women and children, walking along the city streets of Cork, standing, cycling, travelling in trams, play-acting, posing for the camera or simply oblivious to the fact that we can still look at their image on a film long after they have died. The films of Mitchell and Kenyon preserve images of ghosts who once were as real as we, living in the city of Cork. The city centre looks strikingly well. The streets have a prosperous air, and are crowded with people who are busy and seemingly content. At least they seem no less content than we are!

Michael Gough stated that at the end of the nineteenth century many people in Cork still 'lived in houses unfit for human habitation. They rarely had enough food or heat or clothes and lived in lowest-rent dwellings. Famine, emigration, unemployment, failed industry and trade left Cork City in a pitiful state.' I think the evidence suggests that we can form a more positive judgment of life in Cork by the end of Victoria's reign. Significant improvements had been made in the physical environment of the city. Living standards had improved generally, and mortality had fallen considerably. The ordinary people of Cork had come a very long way since 1837, and in 1901 they looked to the future with a confidence that may have been naïve, but was not altogether misplaced.

❧ 9 ❧

MODERN TIMES

There were widespread expectations that Irish freedom would some-how lead to prosperity and an improvement in the quality of people's lives. Such naïve expectations were not easily realised, however, and for much of the twentieth century Cork languished in economic doldrums. There was poverty across much of the city, high unem-ployment and a constant haemorrhage of emigration, until the late 1950s saw the beginnings of a very modest prosperity.

Through the 1960s and '70s there was tremendous confidence in Cork's future, but that was shattered by the traumatic recession of the 1980s, when there were massive job losses in several of Cork's larg-est companies. The problem was compounded by the unprecedented number of school leavers entering the contracting jobs market, resulting in soaring unemployment and another wave of mass emi-gration. Everyone doubted whether we could ever 'catch up' with our neighbours in the rest of the European Union.

The advent of the Celtic Tiger in the 1990s transformed the economic situation dramatically, with sharp increases in employ-ment levels, industrial productivity and general living standards. However, from the early 'noughties', the Irish economy was grow-ing dangerously dependent on a property price bubble that was bound to burst. By the time of the 'credit crunch' of 2008, people in Ireland were enjoying some of the highest incomes or benefits anywhere in the world, but now that the bubble has burst there are years of painful adjustment ahead. Nonetheless, Cork remains far more prosperous now than it had ever been before the Celtic Tiger years. One need only walk down Patrick Street to see something of the transformation of the city. It has the characteristics of a modern, dynamic European city, a city that Corkonians can be more proud of than ever.

THE STRUGGLE FOR INDEPENDENCE

Sagar Mitchell and James Kenyon came to Cork in 1902 to film the Cork International Exhibition organised on the Mardyke by the Lord Mayor of Cork, Edward Fitzgerald. After the exhibition, its grounds were donated to the people of Cork and renamed Fitzgerald's Park. The exhibition was a marvellous showcase for the city and reflected the confidence of Cork's business community at the start of the twentieth century. The well-to-do citizens of Cork were filmed by Mitchell and Kenyon enjoying the spectacle in their very fine clothes, side by side with lesser mortals whose clothes reflected more modest incomes.

While in Cork, Mitchell and Kenyon took the opportunity to film soldiers from the Royal Munster Fusiliers at Victoria Barracks (now Collins Barracks) after their return from fighting for Britain in the Boer War in South Africa. Their film showing a Union Jack flying on Patrick's Street serves as another reminder that Cork was part of the United Kingdom at the start of the twentieth century, and it seemed destined to remain so. When the Great War broke out in August 1914 many Corkmen enlisted in the British army; an estimated 6,000 in all from the city and its environs, of whom about 1,000 were to die in the conflict.

The great majority of the people in Cork were nationalists, but they seem to have believed that Irish nationality could be reconciled with British citizenship under Home Rule. The Irish Volunteers, a paramilitary organisation set up in 1913 to ensure that the British government would grant Ireland Home Rule despite Ulster Unionist opposition, had only 150 members in the city in 1915 who opposed the idea of Irishmen joining Britain's war effort. It was not until after the 1916 Rising that republicanism took hold in Cork. The British military response to the Rising, and growing disenchantment with the impotency of the Home Rule Party, shifted public opinion in favour of a more radical form of nationalist politics. The British government's intention to conscript Irishmen into the British army without their consent antagonised nationalists enormously and paved the way for the Sinn Féin landslide in the general election of December 1918. Sinn Féin sought to win Irish freedom by peaceful means. When that attempt failed, the Irish Republican Army launched the War of Independence.

The National Monument on the Grand Parade was unveiled on St Patrick's Day, 1906. It commemorates the republican rebellions of 1798, 1803, 1848 and 1867. (Courtesy of John Mullins.)

From January 1920, Cork was a city at war. The IRA destroyed the Royal Irish Constabulary barracks at Blackrock, Togher, Victoria Cross, King Street and St Luke's. The RIC were virtually under siege in their headquarters on Union Quay. In March 1920, the RIC were reinforced by the notorious 'Black and Tans', a mercenary police force recruited from the ranks of unemployed British soldiers. On 20 March 1920, a number of police officers broke into the home of Tomás MacCurtain, Lord Mayor of Cork, and shot him dead. A cycle of tit-for-tat killings took place between the IRA and the security forces, which escalated over the course of the months that followed. A very similar pattern of tit-for-tat violence, with British government approval for a policy of 'reprisals' by the security forces, developed in west County Cork, and more generally, if less intensely, across the rest of southern Ireland.

The British government reinforced the RIC further in August 1920 by establishing the Auxiliaries, a paramilitary police force made up of unemployed British army officers. The IRA escalated its campaign by deploying 'flying columns' of large numbers of IRA volunteers who banded together for attacks on the British security forces. Tom Barry's ambush of a convoy of Auxiliaries at Kilmichael, not far from Cork, in which seventeen 'Auxies' and three IRA men were killed, was a spectacular example of a flying column in action. On 11 December 1920, the IRA ambushed an Auxiliary patrol at Dillon's Cross, killing one and wounding twelve others. The Auxiliaries and Black and Tans responded by going on the rampage in Cork's city centre. The city's largest department stores, including the Munster Arcade, Roches Stores, Cash & Co. and Grant & Co., were burned to the ground, along with many smaller premises. The City Hall and the nearby Carnegie Library were also destroyed. Cork was left looking like a Belgian city bombed in the Great War. Nonetheless, the actions of the security forces served only to strengthen republican commitment in what was now 'Rebel Cork'. The IRA campaign intensified

in the months that followed, and, with the assistance of chemists at UCC, a bomb-making factory was set up in the city. However, on 11 July 1921, the British government called a truce and negotiations began for what became the Anglo-Irish Treaty in December 1921.

The Treaty agreed between the British government and the Sinn Féin negotiating team headed by Arthur Griffith and Michael Collins was, inevitably, a compromise. In Collins's words, it gave twenty-six Irish counties not the ultimate freedom that republicans desired, but 'the freedom to achieve it'. The Irish Free State was born. However, most of the IRA in Cork City and county rejected the Treaty. From 28 June 1922, the Free State army fought the anti-Treaty

Tomás MacCurtain, Sinn Féin Lord Mayor of Cork, was murdered by police officers on 20 March 1920. He and his successor, Terence Mac Sweeney, personified 'Rebel Cork' during the War of Independence. (Courtesy of Cork Museum.)

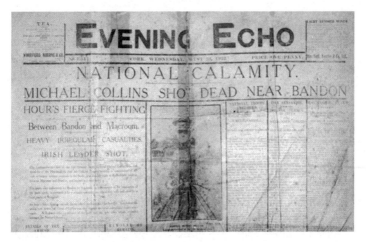

Cork's *Evening Echo* reports the killing of Michael Collins by members of the anti-Treaty IRA in August 1922. (Courtesy of Cork Museum.)

IRA to assert its authority in the new state. The anti-Treaty IRA lacked popular support for their cause, and lacked effective leadership. Within a month of the outbreak of the Irish Civil War only the so-called 'Cork republic' remained in their control. On 8 August 1922, the Irish Free State army landed soldiers from ships at Youghal, Passage and Union Hall. After a battle at Rochestown that left sixteen men dead, the Irish army took control of Cork City on 11 August. The anti-Treaty forces retreated west and fought a savage but short-lived guerrilla war, in which Michael Collins was an early victim. Cork itself remained calm, however, as people were generally war-weary and eager for a return to some kind of normality. In the countryside too, people wanted peace, and in May 1923 the Irish Civil War came to an end. Twenty-six counties enjoyed freedom of a kind, and finally an end to violence.

EARLY CHALLENGES AND RESPONSES

The end of the civil war and the foundation of the Irish state augured a period of new confidence in Cork. In 1923, the Cork Progressives Association was founded to promote the improvement, progress and prosperity of the city. The association was critical of the fact that very

limited progress had been made on rebuilding Cork's city centre
since it had been burnt down by officers of the Black and Tans and
Auxiliaries in 1920. Criticism was made of the poor quality of maintenance of the city's streets, many of which were still paved with timber
blocks. The public water supply was of a poor quality, and refuse disposal in the city was inadequate. There was virtually no building in
progress in the city and the markets were operating at a loss.

The Cork Town Planning Association, founded in 1922 under the
chairmanship of A.F. Sharman Crawford, published a Civic Survey
in 1926 to influence the future development of the city. The survey
identified poor housing as a critical problem, affecting 16,000 people,
or one fifth of the people living within the city boundaries. There
were three concentrations of slums: the largest of them being west
of Shandon Street and north of Blarney Street, with smaller areas in
the 'Marsh' west of Grattan Street and an area off Barrack Street. The
survey recommended that these slums be cleared and their residents
rehoused on the outskirts of the city. The survey also identified traffic
congestion as a problem, caused by the convergence of roads on the
city centre and a lack of bridges. A lack of public open space in Cork
since the industrialisation of Victoria Park from 1917 was identified
as a further problem.

There was a lack of money at the time to do anything about the
traffic or the lack of open space, but the problem of slum housing was
made a priority action point by the City Commissioner and subsequently by the revived Cork Corporation. In 1928, the quality of
the city's water supply, criticised in the enquiry of 1924, was greatly
improved with enhanced filtration and the start of chlorination. In
1928 also, a major public housing scheme of 148 houses was started
at Capwell, between the Cork & Macroom and Cork, Bandon &
South Coast railway lines to the south of the city. Large schemes
were started in nearby Turner's Cross in 1930 and 1932, while in 1934
work began on a large housing scheme at Gurranebraher on Cork's
northside. In 1936 alone, 416 houses were completed for the corporation in schemes across the city. There had been public housing
schemes in Cork since 1886, but nothing on the scale of the corporation's schemes of the 1930s.

The provision of so many corporation houses, and the on-going
clearance of some of the worst slums, improved living conditions in
the city significantly. Public health improved.

Above left: Poor-quality houses, built to high densities with few amenities, such as these cottages off the Bandon Road, were identified as a priority for action by Cork Corporation in the 1920s and '30s. (Courtesy of Cork City Libraries.)

Above right: The church of Christ the King, opened at Turner's Cross in 1931, was one of the 'rosary bead' of Catholic churches built around the new suburbs of Cork from the 1930s. (Courtesy of Cork City Libraries.)

One of the last trains from the CB & PR station at Albert Street. (Photographed by H.C. Casserley in 1932.)

   The city took on a more modern appearance. The electric tram-cars ceased to operate in 1931 and the Irish Omnibus Company provided a public bus service in their steads. Buses also replaced the Cork, Blackrock & Passage Railway in 1932, and the Muskerry railway, which closed in 1934. On the other hand, in 1936, Cork's new, impressive City Hall was officially opened.

Cork's City Hall was opened in 1936, fourteen years after the Black and Tans and Auxiliaries had burnt its predecessor. (Courtesy of Cork City Libraries.)

However, the steady improvement in the physical fabric of Cork belied a fundamental problem in the city – chronic unemployment and its symptoms (poor diet, poor health and poor housing). The city's largest single employer was Fords, set up in 1917. Otherwise, the city's manufacturing sector was dominated by textiles, food and drink processing, and boot and shoe manufacturing, reflecting its continued dependence on its agricultural hinterhand. The Cumann na nGaedhael government looked mainly to agriculture rather than industry to develop the Irish economy. In 1925, work on the Dairy Science Institute was started at University College Cork. However, agriculture failed to generate increased employment on the land or in related industries. Employment in food processing in Cork actually declined. Indeed, Cork showed no gain in manufacturing employment over the first decade of Irish independence. The corporation housing schemes were financed by increased taxation and not by increased wealth.

The coming to power of Fianna Fáil in 1932, against the backdrop of a general move to protectionism across the world during the Depression, augured a change in the Free State's economic policy. De Valera's drive for self-sufficiency was not without a certain logic in the circumstances Ireland found herself in the 1930s, but it was not a policy likely to benefit a port city like Cork, which depended a great deal on international commerce. In fact, the 'economic war' of the mid-1930s inflicted tremendous hardship on Cork by crippling its trade, especially its trade in live cattle to Britain. Between the effects of the Depression, 'self-sufficiency' and the 'economic war', unemployment in Cork soared to a staggering 41.3 per cent in 1936, according to Michael Gough. It was a time of terrible privations within the city.

The ending of the 'economic war' brought only temporary respite in Cork, as Ireland was plunged into the 'Emergency' with the outbreak of the Second World War in 1939. Maritime trade plummeted. Rationing ensured that there was basic provision of food, but unemployment soared once more, reaching almost 45 per cent, according to Gough, by the time the war ended, while real wage levels fell sharply and most of the people in Cork suffered tremendous hardships. The corporation helped by providing allotments for many of the unemployed. Yet poverty and malnutrition led to an increase in the number of people affected by tuberculosis during the war years. There was an outbreak of diptheria and a poliomyelitis epidemic. Not surprisingly, many people from Cork emigrated and the city's population fell by 6 per cent by 1946. Dismal though life was for a great many people in Cork at that time, however, they had at least been spared direct experience of the horrors of the Second World War. Nonetheless, Cork's experience of the first quarter of a century of Irish independence was not at all impressive.

GROWTH AND RECESSION

In 1946, Cork was the commercial and service centre of a large agricultural hinterland. Its great department stores on Patrick Street were far more impressive than the buildings burned down by the Black and Tans. Cork's industries, however, languished badly and poverty prevailed over much of the city. The general post-war economic recovery across western Europe eventually but gradually stimulated economic growth in Ireland also. Car production at Fords was greatly boosted by overseas demand. The surplus land held by Fords was developed into the Marina Industrial Estate, and Gouldings and a new ESB generating station were built there. Exports of agricultural produce grew as demand in Britain increased after the war. There was a general revival of economic life in Cork.

The late 1950s saw major industrial complexes set up in the Cork harbour area. In 1957, the Irish Refining Company was founded and began to refine oil at Whitegate two years later. In 1959, the Verolme Cork Dockyard, an important shipbuilding company, was established at Rushbrooke, near Cóbh. The Irish Steel Plant at Hawlbowline (founded in 1937) was expanded and provided hundreds of jobs in the Greater Cork Area. The year 1961 saw the opening of Cork airport – a major investment in the city's future. The North Gate Bridge was replaced by a very modern Griffith Bridge. There was a real sense that Cork was entering a new economic era. Under Taoiseach Seán Lemass the Irish economy was re-orientated towards world markets. The drive for self-sufficiency was abandoned and considerable efforts were made to attract overseas investment in manufacturing.

One significant reflection of the upturn in Cork's fortunes was the scale of private housing development. M.J. Gough, in tracing the physical expansion of the city, revealed that there was virtually no private house building in Cork in the inter-war years. Apart from the corporation's housing schemes, there were few houses built other than those of the British government's trust for ex-servicemen at Fairhill, at Haig Gardens, off the Boreenmanna Road, and at Whitethorn, off the Douglas Road. The lack of private building shows something of the dire economic straits Cork was in over much of the second quarter of the twentieth century. From the early 1950s, however, there was extensive building of middle-class houses around Cork.

There was very considerable building of private houses around the Douglas Road and South Douglas Road to the south-east of the city, and at Ballinlough and Beaumont, Dennehy's Cross and Wilton. The northside proved to be less popular with private developers, though there was some building at St Anne's Drive and along St Christopher's Road. Cork Corporation built large housing schemes at Ballyphehane and Killeenreendowney on the southside and at Churchfield and Fairfield on the northside. In 1961, Cork City and suburbs had a population of 115,689, a very modest increase over the previous ten years, but in 1971 the population had grown to 134,430. Middle-class houses were built across Bishopstown in the south-west and around Mayfield in the north-east. NBA housing schemes were built at Mayfield and The Glen and at Togher in the late 1960s and early '70s. There was an air of confidence in Cork and the extreme poverty which blighted so many lives in the past was ameliorated.

Patrick Street in 1961.

Given the scale of the physical and economic growth of the city, Cork Corporation commissioned a traffic plan in 1965, published in 1968 as the report on the Cork traffic study. This ambitious report recommended the building of an elevated motorway around the city centre, linked to the main radial routeways, which were to be upgraded to dual-carriageways. Those recommendations sparked off a storm of protest because they would have required the demolition of around 600 homes across the city, and they were unrealistically expensive in any case. The corporation implemented the report's affordable traffic management recommendations, involving a comprehensive one-way traffic system that brought some relief to the city's growing congestion. However, the report's American-style solutions to Cork's traffic problems were simply unacceptable.

The economic growth experienced in the 1960s and the tangible progress achieved across the spectrum of Irish life (much of it reflected on television by RTÉ from 1962), inspired a spirit of tremendous optimism in Cork, which was magnified by the publication of the Buchanan Report in 1968, which advocated the building-up of Cork and Limerick as growth centres to counterbalance the dominance of Dublin. Membership of the European Union (EEC as it was then) was welcomed with great enthusiasm and high expectations. The Harbour Commissioners' 'Cork Harbour Plan' (1972) envisaged a massive increase in port-related industries, and its strategy of developing a major deep-water facility at Ringaskiddy to cater for large-scale capital-intensive industries while directing modern light industries to Little Island, was supported by the Industrial Development Authority (IDA). The Cork Land Use and Transportation Plan, published in 1978, endorsed the Harbour Plan and recommended the development of suburban industrial estates near residential areas in Hollyhill, Togher and Mahon. LUTS projected a two-fold increase in total employment in the Greater Cork Area by 1991 with a consequent increase in population. The IDA invested accordingly in land for industrial estates.

There was a general assumption that Cork's industrial base was strong, and that its splendid harbour, urban infrastructure and young, well-educated pool of available labour would automatically attract new industries. The establishment of Pfizer's large pharmaceutical plant at Ringaskiddy in 1969, and of Apple's major computer manufacturing plant at Hollyhill in 1978, seemed to prove Cork's inherent appeal for multinational investment. The discovery of the large natural gas field in the Celtic Sea resulted in the setting up of a major NÉT fertiliser plant at Marino Point in 1979, the building of a gas-driven ESB power station at Aghada, and the conversion of the ESB station at the Marina to gas power – though the bonanza anticipated for Cork never quite matched expectations.

The face of Cork City was being steadily transformed through the 1970s. A new Parnell Bridge was opened in 1971. Cork Regional Hospital (now Cork University Hospital) opened in 1972. The Cork Regional Technical College (now the Cork Institute of Technology) at Bishopstown followed soon afterwards. The advent of free secondary education resulted in striking increases in the numbers of students remaining at school until the Leaving Certificate, and in the numbers going on to third level education at the rapidly expanding University College Cork and the new Regional College.

Suburban shopping centres were established, first at Douglas in 1971, followed by a smaller centre at Bishopstown. A major shopping centre was built at Wilton in 1979, with a more modest development at Ballyvolane in 1980. In the city centre, too, there were positive developments, with the former Savoy Cinema and the Queen's Old Castle refurbished as shopping arcades. The Munster Arcade closed, but its premises were transformed into a flagship outlet for Penneys. Easons relocated to the former ESB showrooms to secure a strategic location at the heart of Patrick Street. All in all, times seemed very good indeed in Cork until about 1980. Unfortunately, massive government borrowing, much of it spent on a bloated public sector, disguised the reality of considerable weaknesses in the contemporary Irish economy.

Indigenous Irish industries were very vulnerable to increasing foreign competition once Ireland had joined the European Union. The new manufacturing jobs created in Cork city and harbour in the 1970s masked the fact that there was virtually no aggregate gain in industrial employment in the decade. Following the restructuring of the world's economies after the oil crisis, many of Cork's indigenous companies could no longer compete. The LUTS review of 1992 revealed that in the period from 1976 to 1989, the Greater Cork Area lost 68 per cent of its jobs in the clothing and footwear sectors, 38 per cent of jobs in textiles, 42 per cent of jobs in food industries, 23 per cent of jobs in the drinks industries, and 25 per cent of jobs in timber and furniture industries. In all, the Greater Cork Area lost an aggregate of 19 per cent of its manufacturing jobs in that period, with the indigenous sectors bearing the brunt of the losses. Catastrophically, Cork's longstanding 'blue-chip' employers – Ford, Dunlop and Verolme – closed within a twelve-month period in 1983-4, throwing another 2,500 workers onto the dole queues. Cork became an industrial blackspot and the optimism of previous years was completely shattered.

The impact of the 1980s recession was profound, if uneven. The pain inflicted on working-class areas was far greater than that in the middle-class suburbs, where a high proportion of the workforce was employed in the public sector, which was effectively insulated against the threat of redundancy. Young adults of all social backgrounds were hit very hard too. The Irish economy, at local and national levels, was unable to provide more than a fraction of the jobs needed to provide employment for the burgeoning numbers of school leavers and graduates entering the job market throughout the 1980s. The dole queues grew ever longer, despite expedients such as the 'transition year' introduced to secondary schools to help keep thousands off the unemployment registers.

In the 1980s, emigration returned as a feature of Irish life with a vengence. Tens of thousands left Ireland each year to find work elsewhere, particularly in Britain, which enjoyed a boom throughout the mid to late 1980s. Many people who remained in Ireland in the 1980s took some comfort in the notion that the 1980s emigrants were the best-educated exiles ever to leave these shores. It was indeed often the case that the emigrants found employers in other states who appreciated what they had to offer; yet not all Irish emigrants were so fortunate, and for most there was the pain of being sundered from their families, friends and neighbourhoods. There were, then, contrasting experiences of the 1980s recession, between those who, through age or good fortune, kept their jobs and came through the difficult times relatively unscathed, and those whose lives were by transformed by redundancy or exile.

The recession left many derelict premises across Cork, and there were sixteen acres of vacant land in the city centre in 1987. The dereliction was exacerbated by a widespread neglect of the physical appearance of the city, as the amount of money allocated for street maintenance and street cleaning was reduced. Second-hand stores proliferated and there was a general air of poverty and decline in the central parts of Cork. Recent exiles visiting family and friends were frequently struck by how 'run-down' Cork had become in those dismal years.

CELTIC TIGER

The 1980s recession stripped away virtually all of Cork's uncompetitive companies. By the end of the decade the number of job losses fell sharply, while there was an increase in the number of new jobs being created. UCC's National Microelectronics Research Centre and the IDA's High Technology Business Park considerably enhanced Cork's attractiveness to multinational computer companies. Apple was joined by Western Digital, Bournes Electronics, Motorola and a series of similar companies in the city's suburban industrial estates, and especially at Bishopstown, which boasts the greatest concentration of electronics firms in the Greater Cork Area. Ringaskiddy's deep-water facilities and related infrastructure were finally put in place and Pfizer and Penn Chemicals were joined by Sandoz, Johnson & Johnson and by SmithKline Beecham, among others, to create the greatest concentration of pharmaceutical firms in Ireland. There was a revival in the indigenous industrial sector too, with new start-ups in all of the suburban industrial estates, and in the redeveloped Marina Industrial Estate.

Cork's undoubted attractions for modern industrial development were bolstered by the state's offering of very low corporate tax rates to encourage multinational investment. It was also helped greatly by the availability of a very large pool of well-educated young adults who were desperate for employment and prepared to accept very 'competitive' wage levels. Industrial growth in Cork was significantly facilitated by improvements in the city's infrastructures, most visibly in the impressive upgrading of the arterial roads leading to and from the city, in the building of the new link roads around the city and the Jack Lynch Tunnel under the Lee (opened in 1999). In 1989, the Cork–Swansea car-ferry service was revived. Cork Airport has seen expansion in its passenger numbers and in its physical capacity. The railways began seeing major investment after years of neglect. Telecommunications were upgraded, and continue to be upgraded, in line with the requirements of modern consumers. Even the sewers were modernised.

The industrial boom which began at the end of the 1980s proved to be the catalyst for remarkable economic growth – averaging 10 per cent and more in some years – which closed the gap in GNP per capita between Ireland and the richer states of the European

Union by the end of the millennium. Ireland's dependency ratio fell
dramatically as the birth rate tumbled and the unemployed found
gainful employment. There were significant numbers of emigrants
who returned to Ireland in the 1990s with skills and invaluable
experience gained in countries around the world, and there was significant immigration into Ireland for the first time in centuries. As
the Celtic Tiger economy went from strength to strength, Ireland's
punitively high levels of taxation were pared back, interest rates fell
as the punt converged with the other European currencies which
would adopt the euro in 2002, disposable incomes increased considerably, and there was a very real improvement in average living
standards.

Already in 1985 there was a modestly sized city-centre shopping
development at Paul Street which acted as a catalyst for the revi-
talisation of a decayed part of the city adjacent to Patrick Street.
Pedestrianisation of adjoining streets and the redevelopment of derelict or under-utilised properties into restaurants, book shops, etc.,
created an attractive environment which has been designated as the
'Huguenot Quarter'. Princes Street, Winthrop Street, Cook Street
and Marlborough Street, linking Patrick Street with Oliver Plunkett
Street (the city's second most important shopping street), were all
pedestrianised to enhance their appeal to shoppers.

The success of the Paul Street development, and the beginnings of
economic revival, encouraged the establishment of the Merchant's
Quay Shopping Centre on Patrick Street in 1989. This major investment brought new dynamism and confidence to retailing in Cork's
city centre. In 1990, Douglas Court Shopping Centre was opened
beside the South Link Road at Douglas, while Bishopstown Court
was opened at the western end of the Link Road in 1994. The major
shopping centres recently established at Blackpool and Mahon also
reflected the strong attraction of improved road communications for
retail investment. Increasing prosperity allowed for the expansion
of retailing in both the city centre and the suburbs. The city centre
especially reflected the novel affluence created by the Celtic Tiger,
with striking increases in the number of women's fashion outlets, and
in the number of travel agents. A Virgin Megastore and HMV outlet
were also established in the city centre. Unfortunately, as car owner-
ship increased so too did the problem of congested streets, one of the
greatest environmental challenges still facing the city.

Above left: Since the completion of Cork's state-of-the-art sewage treatment system, the River Lee in the city centre has been developed as a major amenity. This photograph shows the Lee boardwalk facing Sullivan's Quay. (Courtesy of John Mullins.)

Above right: Opera Lane, between Patrick Street and the Crawford Art Gallery, experienced massive redevelopment at the start of the twenty-first century. (Courtesy of John Mullins.)

One of the more interesting developments in Cork in the 1990s was the Historic Centre Action Plan commissioned by Cork Corporation in 1992 and supported by the European Union's Conservation of European Cities Programme. The plan was focused on Cork's historic core area, the formerly walled area around the North and South Main Streets, the areas around Shandon Street and Barrack Street, and some adjoining districts. A north–south spine for development, ranging from St Anne's Cathedral in the north across the island to St Fin Barre's Cathedral in the south, has been identified, together with a west–east spine from the splendid Cork Museum in Fitzgerald's Park on the Mardyke through Corn Market Street and Paul Street to the Crawford Art Gallery and Opera House at Emmet Square. It is intended to develop the potential of this core area to contribute to the cultural and economic life of the city.

There was a general awareness of the importance of Cork's historic centre, but little evidence of Cork's medieval past survived above street level. The corporation appointed a city archaeologist to help to develop our knowledge and appreciation of Cork's archaeological heritage. The first phase of the plan, the Urban Pilot Project, concentrated on improving the physical environment of the North Main Street which had been neglected and become run-down, and on stimulating economic activity in the area. The North Main Street was resurfaced and attractive footpaths were put in place along the street and in Castle Street and Daunt's Square. There are brass plaques celebrating each of the medieval lanes leading off the Main Street. A major excavation project was financed at the North Gate, and the Cork Vision Centre was established in the former St Peter's church on the North Main Street as an educational and promotional facility for the historic centre of Cork. The main catalyst for economic regeneration is the North Main Street Shopping Centre, together with a cinema complex, hostel and apartments. Many small shops have become established in the area, and the overall result is a significant transformation of that part of the historic centre of Cork. The Historic Centre Action Plan is certainly ambitious, in that it aspires to regenerating a very extensive portion of Cork, but the progress achieved to date has certainly been impressive and promising.

CONCLUSION

At the start of the third millennium, Cork has the air of a vibrant, dynamic and prosperous city. Massive investment in manufacturing, retailing and a host of services have transformed the face of the city, and urban renewal has brought life to formerly neglected corners of the city, not just through the Historic Centre Action Plan discussed above but through the large-scale building of private apartments, like those overlooking the Lee at Clarke's Bridge. The population of Cork's city centre actually increased during the 1990s, after more than a century of continuous decline. By 2000 almost a quarter of a million people were living in the Greater Cork Area. In 2005, Cork was designated as the European Capital of Culture, a great honour but one which was well deserved.

The city is not without problems. Traffic congestion continues to clog its streets. There is still a lot of work to do in improving the physical fabric of extensive parts of the historic centre of the city. The Celtic Tiger did not eliminate poverty completely from Cork.

Patrick Street, Cork, in 2010. (Courtesy of John Mullins.)

The 'over-heating' of the economy during the last of the Tiger years resulted in grossly inflated house prices, and over-pricing for most commodities. Now that the bubble has burst, property prices are falling back towards more realistic levels, and there is a great consciousness of the need to regain price competitiveness in external markets, especially for indigenous Irish firms. Nonetheless, in Cork's long history, stretching back to the foundation of the monastery attributed to St Finbarr, through the Middle Ages and up to contemporary times, the people of Cork have never 'had it so good' as they do now. Once the current phase of economic adjustment is completed, the prospects for the future remain very promising indeed.

BIBLIOGRAPHY

Cleary, Rose M. & Hurley, Maurice F., *Cork city excavations: 1984-2000* (Cork City Council: Cork, 2003).

Cronin, Maura, *Country, class or craft: the politicisation of the skilled artisan in 19th century Cork* (Cork University Press: Cork:, 1994).

Crowley, J.S., R.J.N. Devoy, D. Linehan & P. O'Flanagan (eds), *Atlas of Cork city* (Cork University Press: Cork, 2005).

D'Alton, Ian, *Protestant society and politics in Cork, 1812-1844* (Cork University Press: Cork, 1980).

Dickson, David, *Old world colony: Cork and south Munster, 1630-1830* (Cork University Press: Cork, 2005).

Jefferies, Henry Alan, *Cork: historical perspectives* (Four Courts Press: Dublin, 2004).

McCarthy, Mark, 'Geographical change in an early modern town: urban growth, economy and cultural politics in Cork, 1600-1641' in *Journal of the Cork Historical & Archaeological Society*, vol. 106 (2001).

Murphy, John A., *The College: a history of Queen's/University College Cork 1845-1995* (Cork University Press: Cork, 1995).

O'Flanagan, Patrick, Cornelius Buttimer & Gerard O'Brien (eds), *Cork: history and society* (Geography Publications: Dublin, 1993).

O'Sullivan, William, *The economic history of Cork city: from the earliest times to the Act of Union* (Cork University Press: Cork, 1937).

Pettit, Seán, *This City of Cork, 1700-1900* (Studio Publications: Cork, 1977).

Rynne, Colin, *The archaeology of Cork city and harbour: from the earliest times to industrialisation* (Collins Press: Cork, 1993).

Smith, Charles, *The ancient and present state of the county and city of Cork* (Guy & Co.: Cork, 1893).

Windele, John, *Historical and descriptive notices of the city of Cork and its vicinity* (Bolster: Cork, 1846).

LIBRARIES
LEABHARLANNA

CORK CITY COUNCIL | COMHAIRLE CATHRACH CHORCAÍ

CORK PAST AND PRESENT
www.corkpastandpresent.ie

'Cork Past and Present' is an online service of Cork City Libraries, providing information on Cork's history, culture, places, people, and events. The site focuses on Cork City and its surrounding areas, providing new textual material as well as digital images, including local photographs, drawings, maps, and advertisements. This continually expanding site, which began in 2004, has approximately 200 pages and about 300 images.

The following is a summary list of useful information on this site:

- Historical maps of Cork City.
- Photographs of city and environs, from 1860 to the present, with accompanying information.
- Cork-related images and OCR-text from *The Irish Builder* (1867–84) and *The Illustrated London News* (1842–58).
- Outline history of the development of Cork City.
- Bilingual list of 1,400 city street names.
- Bilingual list of townlands in or near Cork City.
- Bilingual list of local geographical features.
- Old advertisements from city-centre businesses.
- Business-directory extracts for Patrick's Street between 1787 and 1997.
- Map of the Patrick's Street area, containing hypertext links.
- Lists of historic and current newspapers available in Cork City Libraries.
- Guide to tracing family roots in the Cork region.
- Links to useful current information about Cork.